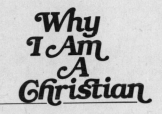

Why I Am A Christian

"A word to honest doubters"

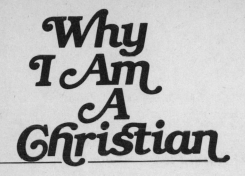

Why I Am A Christian

O. Hallesby

Translated by Clarence J. Carlsen

AUGSBURG PUBLISHING HOUSE
MINNEAPOLIS, MINNESOTA

WHY I AM A CHRISTIAN

Manufactured in the United States of America

Preface

EVER since I was delivered from doubt and translated into a peaceful and happy life with God, I have felt indebted to my doubting fellow men. This book is an attempt to pay off some of that debt. I have not succeeded so well as I had earnestly desired that I might; but since so little in our devotional literature has been written for the purpose of aiding the doubter, I have, nevertheless, ventured to send it forth. It is my prayer to God that it may find its way into the hands of some doubter who will not despise what little help I might be able to give.

O. HALLESBY.

Vinderen, Norway.

Contents

BOOK ONE

Doubt

IN SO FAR as we mortals dare venture an opinion concerning the invisible realities of life, it can be said with certainty that never have there been as many believers in our country as there are now. But neither have there been as many doubters.

A generation or two ago this was quite otherwise. Then there were only a very few doubters. All the rest believed in the truth of Christianity, accepted the Bible as the word of God, and Christ as God.

Now, however, doubt is more common than many suspect, among the educated as well as among those whose knowledge is very limited.

Some folk view our age with dark misgivings because of the skepticism which prevails. And it is true: doubt is more than terrible mental distress; it is an internal cancer, which eats away the vitality of the nation as well as that of the individual. However, we should bear in mind that much of the faith in the Bible and in Christianity which formerly existed was of little value. It had been taken over from the environment, in most instances without a personal experience of salvation, and was, consequently, impersonal and traditional.

It is conceded that this traditional faith in the Word of God possessed a certain value, both to the individual and to the nation. Undoubtedly it put a damper upon ungodliness. On the other hand, we must bear in mind that no one is saved merely by holding the Bible to be the Word of God. We now see clearly how impersonal and impotent this "faith" was. By far the greater number simply took over their faith from their environment. A changed environment, therefore, was all that was necessary in order to undermine their "faith." As soon as the environment began to sow the seeds of doubt in their hearts by means of the daily press, literature, popular science, etc., it became apparent that a large proportion of our people was quite defenseless.

By heritage, training, and tradition most of them, no doubt, desired to retain their "faith." But they simply could not. They were not prepared to meet doubt.

Further reflection will make this very clear to us.

The Christian truths, like all religious and moral truths, are of such a nature that it is impossible to demonstrate them in the same way in which a proposition in mathematics or physics can be demonstrated. The mathematical, logical, and general historical truths are of such a nature that every normal, intelligent person must accept them. Moral and religious truths, on the other hand, are not necessarily valid to every thinking person. Only by living in the realm of morality and religion can a person become cognizant of the validity of moral and religious truths.

It is difficult for a man who does not live a moral life to feel the validity of moral truths. He will readily doubt even such an elementary truth as the qualitative difference between right and wrong. Religion too becomes unreal to the man who does not live a religious life.

This is especially applicable with reference to the Christian truths. No portion of reality involves so many intellectual difficulties and has so many incomprehensible aspects as Christianity. If a person does not know Christian life from personal experience, intellectual difficulties will quickly make him skeptical of Christianity.

As soon as their environment becomes antagonistic toward Christianity, these people, having no weapons, are unable to defend themselves. Let us illustrate briefly.

People say: "There are so many religions. How is it possible to know that Christianity is absolutely the only true one?"

If you should answer naively and confidently: "The Bible says so," the other would promptly reply: "Very well, but what of it? The Koran, the Bible of the Muhammedans, says that Islam is the only true religion."

If you answer again: "Yes, but the Bible is the Word of God," the other will say: "How do you know?"

"Everybody has told me that—my father, my mother, my teacher, and my pastor."

"Well, how do they know that the Bible is the Word of God?"

"They have been told so by their fathers and mothers, pastors and teachers. Furthermore, the whole church teaches that the Bible is the Word of God."

"Yes, but the church is made up of human beings. They are fallible."

"But the apostles who wrote the New Testament say that it is the Word of God."

"True enough, but they, too, were only human. They no doubt meant what they said and wrote, and they finally gave their lives for their faith; but who can guarantee that they did not deceive themselves and that they were not mistaken? That has happened to well-meaning and credulous people both before that time and since.

"Furthermore, as you know, all the higher religions have their sacred writings, which their followers believe to be from God, and therefore, the Word of God. By what right are the sacred writings of Christianity accorded an exclusive place? Ought we not rather put them all on the same plane and assume that none of them is of divine origin, especially since they are mutually contradictory and can not, therefore, all be from God? It is most reasonable to presume that none of them is of God.

"Most likely the origin of all of them can be traced to individuals who believed, each within his own religion, that what they wrote was a direct revelation to them from God.

"An examination of the contents of these sacred writings makes this still more apparent. This applies to the sacred scriptures of the Christians as well as to the others.

"In the first place, there are mistakes and inconsistencies in the Bible. If it were the Word of God, ought it not at least be inerrant?

"Furthermore, the Bible contains many thoughts that are human and imperfect to the highest degree and can not, therefore, be divine. It speaks about a God who has become so angry because of man's sin that He can not pardon before He sees blood. And if He can not get the blood of the guilty, He takes that of the innocent.

"It says also that God is triune, i. e., that there are three eternal persons in God: Father, Son, and Spirit. And yet there are not three Gods, but one.

"It says that only a few are saved. All the rest God condemns to eternal suffering. These must be human thoughts about God; because if God is perfect love, He can not punish any one forever. Not even a human being would do anything as horrible as that, even towards his worst enemy.

"And note all the things that are said about Christ. He is God and man in one person. He is conceived of the Holy Spirit and born of a virgin. He died vicariously for the sins of the whole race. He arose bodily the third day after His death.

"It was thought formerly that this was absolutely unique and that the Bible alone contained such accounts. But modern research in the field of comparative religion has shown that similar things are told also about the founders of other religions. All students of the subject agree that these accounts must be looked upon as myths and legends, which arose in a natural way about these great religious personalities. By what scientific right can the corresponding accounts about Jesus be put in a class by themselves?

"In general it can be said that the supernatural miracle constitutes the one great difficulty in the Christian faith and philosophy of life. . . .

"The difficulty in connection with the miracle is this: No science today recognizes the miracle, neither natural science, historical science, nor the science of comparative religion. Still worse is this: The dominant scientific thought of our day not only denies the reality of the miracle, but also its very possibility. That is axiomatic in this scientific method. It declares outright that the miracle is incompatible with scientific research.

"Modern historical research, for instance, says that every historical source which contains accounts of miracles must on that ground alone be considered only a second-rate source, even if it otherwise has all the distinctive characteristics of a primary source.

"The same science says, further, that everything is relative, that is, finite. Therefore there is no such a thing as absolute truth, as maintained by Christianity. Every historical truth wears the garb of its own day, and must be changed and improved upon as time passes and development progresses. The Christian truths must subject themselves to similar alterations.

"Present day science says also that everything is relative; therefore no *unicum*, nothing absolutely unique, exists, either in nature or in history. For that reason Christ can not be absolutely unique either. Everything has an analogy; Christ, too, must have one.

"That Christ should be the Perfect Man, not to speak of the God-man, as maintained by Christianity, is, therefore, a scientific impossibility.

"In order to gain a scientific appreciation of Christ, we must resolutely divest Him of everything absolute and unique and, by means of the scientific principle of analogy, put Him in the category in which He belongs, among the other religious geniuses whom we are accustomed to designate as founders of religions."

— — —

Every one who has to some degree felt the force of these intellectual difficulties asks: Is it possible to reconcile Christian faith with scientific thought?

To many this becomes an unhappy dilemma, from which they know no other way of escape than by brutally cutting the Gordian knot. Some choose science and bid farewell to Christianity. Others choose faith and throw scientific thought overboard.

In both groups there are, no doubt, many who wish they were back in the simple faith of their childhood or that of the uneducated, undisturbed by reflection.

BOOK TWO

From Doubt to Faith

THERE are two kinds of doubters.

First, there are those who love to doubt, because their skepticism shields them from the accusations of conscience. They will not give up the selfish life they are living, either in coarse and open sins, in ordinary love of the world, or in the self-sufficiency of outward morality. When their conscience disturbs them, doubt is the best means they have of pacifying it.

That is why we see people defending their skepticism as a precious possession, with which they would not part. They select literature which strengthens their doubt. They seize every opportunity to debate questions pertaining to Christianity. Even if they do not succeed in convincing their opponent in debate, they themselves at least feel more secure every time they have been able to bewilder their believing opponent and drive him to the wall.

I would like to say at once to every doubter of this type who may happen to be reading this little book: It is not to you that I venture to proffer my help.

You wish to debate. You expect me to take up all these questions for discussion. But I shall not do that. I do not believe that argumentation is the way to overcome doubt. The doubt of which we are speaking here can not be overcome by logical arguments.

Experience alone can lead our souls from doubt to certainty.

The doubters to whom I venture to proffer my help are of a different description.

They are in distress because of their doubt. They are tired of painful uncertainty. They long for the peaceful rest which calm and impregnable assurance affords.

But every time they think they have found solid ground upon which to stand, they sink back again into the bottomless sea of doubt.

Their inner uncertainty becomes even more distressing to them whenever they come in touch with friends and companions who have found God.

To the latter, God is no longer a problem, the unrealized object of their thinking, seeking, and longing. To them, God is a living reality. They have experienced God. Theirs is the assurance of experience with its peace, joy, and power.

*

It is to these sincere, seeking, but distressed doubters that I venture to offer my assistance.

I, too, have passed through the various stages of doubt. I have felt its anguish. But I also know a way out of doubt and into faith, a way which is open to all doubters. And this way does not do violence to any of our human faculties, not even to our reasoning powers.

This way was pointed out by Jesus over 1900 years ago. He put it in these words: "If any man willeth to do His will, he shall know of the teaching, whether it is of God, or whether I speak from Myself" (John 7:17).

Here He promises to give personal assurance on the

basis of experience. He names only one condition: if any man willeth to do God's will.

In these words Jesus tells us something very important about doubt and the cause of doubt. Many are of the opinion that the cause of their doubt is their great knowledge or the keenness of their intellects. Others are more modest and think that their doubt is due to the fact that they lack knowledge and do not have a sufficiently keen intellect.

It is due to none of these. The cause of your doubt is something entirely different. You lack certain experiences. That is why you find yourself in doubt and uncertainty.

In offering you my help to overcome doubt, I shall not meet your doubts with logical arguments. I shall rather, as well as I can, point out the experiences through which you must pass in order to cope successfully with doubt. At the same time I shall try to indicate the course you must pursue in order to gain these experiences.

If you will follow this course and thus gain these experiences, you will find that your experiences themselves will dispel your doubts. Life itself will do it in its own simple way.

*

My first bit of advice is this: *Read the New Testament.*

Indeed, you say, if I could only believe what it says, I would be helped. But it is the very message of the Bible about which I am in doubt. I do not deny the Bible. On the contrary, I desire to be a believer, but I can not make myself believe. I doubt it instead of believing it.

To this I would reply: I know that such is your

condition. I am well acquainted with it and shall not take too much for granted.

I presuppose that you doubt the supernatural origin of Scripture and likewise that you doubt most, perhaps all, of the miraculous accounts in the New Testament. Nevertheless, I ask you to read the New Testament.

Jesus never required His listeners to accept and beforehand approve of a greater or lesser number of dogmas about Himself. He urged them rather to come to Him, hear His voice, and follow Him.

What happened? All who honestly did so, experienced Jesus and soon became personally convinced of the truth of what He said about Himself. When they later gave expression to that which they had experienced and of which they had become personally assured, the result was the New Testament Scriptures.

Read this marvelous collection of writings and you will see how remarkably the statements of these various authors concerning Jesus coincide.

Since that time millions of people have met Christ and experienced His wonderful person; and when they desire to give expression to that which they have experienced and of which they have become certain, they can find no better words than those which are used in the New Testament.

After a while these people felt the need of expressing in short statements the main substance of what they had experienced when they met Christ. These sentences are called church confessions. Of these I would mention first and foremost the Apostolic Creed, because it is held in common by all Christian church bodies in the world.

Note the facts with regard to the doctrines which this common confession of the church contains. These doctrines are not set forth by the church as something which the individual must accept. The dogmas do, however, give expression to those things with reference to Christ of which an individual does become certain when he experiences Him as his Saviour.

Jesus has always, now as nineteen hundred years ago, named only one condition upon which He will help us to gain personal assurance. And that one condition is this: "If any man willeth to do God's will, . . ."

*

Now take your New Testament and read it for the purpose of ascertaining the "will of God."

But, you say, it is so difficult for me to read the New Testament. All the accounts of miracles and many other questionable thoughts and expressions distract and even offend me and make it difficult for me to read with a calm and open mind.

My friend, I remember this well from the time when I was a doubter. My advice to you is that you omit reading, for the time being, everything which is too offensive to your intellect. Read the remainder. It is fully sufficient to help you out of doubt and into personal assurance with respect to the Christ and the whole Scriptural testimony concerning Him.

Even if you omit the things I have mentioned, you will find on practically every page of the New Testament something which you must without doubt recognize as the "will of God." By that I mean eternal truths, independent of time, place, and persons; as true today as in the time of Christ, as true at the North Pole as at the Equator, as true and eternally applicable with reference to kings as to beggars.

Permit me at this point to mention just one such

saying of Jesus: "All things therefore whatsoever ye would that men should do unto you, even so do ye also unto them" (Matthew 7:12).

Do this, Jesus says.

You will now understand better perhaps why I said in the foregoing that I do not expect to help any other doubters than those who are in distress because of their doubt and who desire, if possible, to escape from it, regardless of cost.

To do unto others whatsoever you would that they should do unto you is no mere child's play, no lazy man's task. Jesus says: Do it! That means: Do not only think about it, speak about it, debate it, long for it, and dream about it; do it.

Note the words of Jesus: "If any man willeth to do His will, he shall know of the teaching, whether it is of God, or whether I speak from myself."

If you will begin to do this, you will gain some entirely new experiences, experiences which will help you out of doubt and into personal assurance. The reason that people doubt Christianity is simply this: They only think about it instead of living it. "The life is the light of men" (John 1:4). In the darkness of doubt also it is life, the living of life itself, which brings light.

Permit me to outline briefly the experiences you will have.

If you begin seriously and earnestly to do unto others as you would have them do unto you, you will experience, in the first place, that you do not do it. Not for one day, not for a half day, not even for an hour do you do unto others as you would have them do unto you.

In the second place, you will experience that you can not do it. You are not able to do it.

In the third place, you will experience that the reason you are unable to do it is simply that you do not desire to do it. It is too irksome, too unprofitable, too painful. After you have tried to do it several times in succession, you get tired of it and slip back into your usual life of comfort and ease, following the well known proverb: Each man for himself first.

If you are sincere, you will have found in your experience, in the fourth place, that you are evil. You feel the moral truth in the statement of Jesus that men are evil, and you are inwardly convinced that your way of acting is morally reprehensible; but you continue to lead a selfish life, nevertheless, in spite of your most sacred convictions, because you desire to avoid the effort, the sacrifice, and the suffering involved in doing the right thing.

You are now ready for more new experiences.

You will, in the fifth place, experience how dishonest you are in the midst of your selfishness. You desire very much to have people believe that you are not selfish. You are glad when people misunderstand you and think that you are performing an act of self-sacrifice, when your own inner self tells you that selfishness is the impelling motive. When you have done a selfish and evil deed which has come to the knowledge of men, you notice how you try in every way to make your act appear laudable, or excuse it in order to make men believe that you did not do it for selfish reasons but with good intentions, or, at worst, that you did it in foolishness or thoughtlessness. To admit that you were selfish is much harder for you than to admit that you were foolish, although the latter also may be hard enough.

In the sixth place, you will experience that you are not true to yourself. You begin to notice now that you also try to represent your own acts to yourself in a better light than truth would permit. You employ many arts and artifices in order to pacify your troubled conscience. If you have spread evil report about somebody, you excuse yourself by saying that what you said was at least true. If you have told a lie, you excuse yourself by saying that it was a "white lie." You consider that permissible. If you have been angry or sulky, you either blame others or attribute it to your temperament.

If you have had these simple but fundamental moral experiences, you have become personally convinced that Jesus was right when he deliberately characterized us in these words: "Ye . . . being evil" (Luke 11:13).

Without doubt, this evaluation of us human beings by Jesus has hitherto been a thorn in your eye. You have felt it as an exaggeration and therefore not true. With many other superficial people you have said: "Men are not so bad after all. There is much good in all of us."

You are now through with such superficial thinking. Nobody needs to force you now to believe the words of Jesus: "Ye . . . being evil." You are personally certain of the truth of this "dogma." You are so thoroughly convinced that even though all the "optimists" in the world might deny these words of Jesus, it would not alter in the least the certainty which you now possess.

If you have followed this advice and read the New Testament, Jesus will stand before you in a new light. Morally, you have become mature enough to see the uniqueness of the person of Jesus.

You see now with new eyes that Jesus during his whole life did unto others whatsoever He would that they should do unto Him. Jesus actually lived this out during His entire life. He did it; He did not only talk about it.

You knew before that Jesus was the noblest man known to history. But it did not really make much of an impression upon you. Now, on the other hand, you have the moral qualifications for evaluating this aspect of Jesus.

Indeed, you now discover that that perfect mind which was in Jesus is the most incomprehensible thing about Him. From the experiences you have had with your own selfish life and your own evil mind you have become psychologically or, rather, morally qualified to evaluate the absolute uniqueness of His human life.

After you yourself have tried to do unto others as you would have them do unto you, and have not succeeded in doing so for even one whole day, you ask yourself: After all, who was Jesus, who was able to do this very thing throughout a whole lifetime—without a single misstep or mistake and in such a natural and matter of fact way, as though there were no other way of living life?

You now have the inner qualifications for experiencing the miraculous in the person of Jesus. The real miraculous, the real supernatural aspect of Jesus is His mind of absolute goodness. Here you are face to face with the supernatural, the absolute. You are now in possession of an inner, direct, personal assurance concerning the most unique miracle in our universe. Can you prove that the mind of Jesus was supernatural? Can I prove it to you?

No; but remember that I said at the very beginning that doubt can not be overcome by logical arguments, but by experience only. All I promised you was that I would point out the experiences you would have to go through in order to rid yourself of doubt and receive personal assurance.

And that is what I have done. When you, with your own moral experience, stand before Jesus as He is presented to us in the New Testament, as I in the foregoing have outlined, you will, as millions before you have done, experience the mind of Jesus as a miracle, a supernatural mind.

Note now that you can become assured of this miracle, this fundamental miracle with respect to Jesus, even though you still doubt the miracles which it is said Jesus performed.

*

Your skepticism is now really doomed. It will not be long until you will be rid of all your doubts.

When a person has *experienced* something of the miraculous, the brunt of his difficulties in connection with miracles is broken. This follows according to the laws of psychology. There are many things which to us seem self-contradictory and absurd as long as we only think and speculate about them. But as soon as we experience them the inconsistency vanishes. It may be impossible for us for some time to come to explain all of our experiences, but all inconsistency has disappeared because of the very fact that we have experienced these things. Our mind is so constituted that it submits to the facts of experience even while it is still unable to think through or explain the experience.

If somebody had said a generation ago that some day it would be possible to sit in a remote nook in Finnmarken and hear a divine service conducted in Our Savior's Church in Oslo, people would have said that such a thing was absurd and inconceivable. Now no one says anything about the impossibility of it.

As long as our minds have no experiences to build

upon, we feel compelled to declare things inconceivable. But as soon as our minds have experienced actual facts, our whole intellectual basis is changed, and inconsistencies and absurdities vanish.

So also with the miracle.

So long as we only think about the miracle, it appears inconceivable and absurd. But when we experience the miracle, we have actual facts with which to deal and our mental attitude with respect to the miracle is changed. Confronted with experience, the mind withdraws its previous protest and begins its usual work, that of assembling and co-ordinating the facts of experience and classifying them in their proper place among other experiences, as far as this is possible.

*

If you have experienced that miraculous aspect of Jesus which is fundamental, namely, that His inner being is different from that of all the rest of us, that He, according to His ethical nature, is essentially different from all other people, you have also reached a new position with regard to the other miraculous aspects of His life and person.

Here, too, your intellectual difficulties will gradually disappear. A great deal which formerly seemed absurd to you will now become self-evident and natural. And that in spite of the fact that you can by no means explain everything.

Let us look at this for a moment.

If you have experienced that Jesus according to His inner, ethical nature is essentially different from all other men, it is no longer an inconsistency to your mind, but, on the contrary, something very reasonable when the New Testament states that He has a different origin from all the rest of us. Neither is it an inconsistency to our minds when He Himself says that He existed before His life on earth—as the eternal Son of God.

If such is the case, neither is it an inconsistency that His birth took place in a manner different from ours. When the New Testament says that He became incarnate by a creative act of God's own Spirit, our minds say : that is only natural ; that is the way it had to be.

And if there is a fundamental difference between His inner, ethical person and ours, it can not be an inconsistency when the New Testament says that He is endowed with power different from any that we have. Why should He not by means of this power be able to intervene both in the spiritual as well as in the natural realm? If He is in possession of a power different from any which we possess and by means of which He governs His own person, why should He not be able to deal with the natural world in a way different from that in which we are able to deal with it?

Moreover, if He is in possession of a unique inner life, it can not be an inconsistency when the New Testament says that in death, too, He was different from us, in that He broke the usual bonds of death and arose bodily from the grave on the third day.

In a similar way I could go through all the miracles which we are told Jesus performed, but it would take us too far afield. Let me, therefore, only point out again that it is my personal experience of the miraculous element in the person of Jesus which has given me a new attitude with regard to the various other miraculous accounts. It is only in connection with the person of Jesus that these miracles become plausible—I might almost say self-evident.

My next bit of advice is this: Begin to pray to God.
Begin at the same time as you begin to read the New
Testament.

But I doubt the value of prayer, you say.

Yes, I know that. But begin nevertheless.

Then I will be praying without being perfectly sincere
about it, and that will never do, you say.

There is where you make a mistake. To pray does
not mean that you are to begin to offer such prayers as
you hear others pray, your father or mother or pastor,
for instance. To do so would certainly be insincerity on
your part, and that will never do. Insincerity in one's
relationship to God is more dangerous than any other
kind of insincerity.

Nay; but to pray is to speak candidly and confidentially
with God. Why can you not do that even though you
are a doubter? You speak with human beings; why
should you not speak with God, the Highest Being? He
is invisible, it is true; but is not the real person in men
also invisible? That which is visible to your eye is only
flesh and blood. You must believe that they have an
inner being and by faith establish contact with that being
and thus become certain of their being!

Very well, but what shall I say when I pray, you
ask.

You are to speak candidly and confidentially with God.
Begin, therefore, by telling Him the truth, that you are
in doubt about Him and that you do not believe in prayer.
Ask Him to draw near unto you and speak with you in
order that your doubts may be removed and that you may
become certain of Him and certain that He hears your
prayers.

I am prepared to hear someone say: I have tried to pray, but not with the result of which you speak. I have received no answer. And I have prayed very earnestly. I cried to God the time my mother was struggling with death, the time my own child lay writhing in pain. In my distress I cried to God to intervene and help them out of pain and me out of doubt, that I might be certain that He is and that He hears and answers when we human beings pray. But there was no answer. And that was the greatest disappointment of my life, you add disconsolately.

*

With this, too, I am well acquainted. The experience you have had is not new to me. When I was a doubter, I had a similar experience. Permit me to tell a little about it; perhaps it will be of some help to you.

For a long time I was an irreligious doubter. I thought that if there were a personal God, He did not concern himself about each and every individual. However, the more I studied the religious history of the human race, the clearer it became to me that religion is a phase of human soul-life which resides inherently in man in the same way as poetry and music, and which will not permit itself to be removed from life.

I observed that there were, indeed, irreligious individuals, but not irreligious peoples. I observed, further, that the irreligious individual is an artificial product, found only among sophisticated and hyper-cultured people in divers periods, especially periods of decadence. I also saw that this artificial product was the result of the suppression of innate religious tendencies, either on the part of the parents of the children while the children were still young, or on the part of individuals themselves at a more mature age. In the latter instance the suppression was accomplished, as a rule, by great effort, the individual quelling his religious feelings and longings by means of a so-called intellectual or scientific view of life.

I observed, furthermore, that even in irreligious individuals the inherent religious desires are so strong that sophistication must give way to nature. The religious longings of these people often protrude through their "intellectual" unbelief.

Moreover, I saw that religion does not by any means degrade an individual. On the contrary, I was forced to admit that religion is the most exalting element in all human history, even though in exceptional instances it has been corrupted and therefore has less successfully accomplished its purpose.

I observed that nations were sound and strong as long as their religions were vital, and that they became unfitted for life when religion became an empty form to most of their people.

And I saw, further, that the religious individuals were the noblest our race had produced, and that in religion they possessed a means of elevating others which I could not find elsewhere.

*

These and similar reflections opened the way for the innate religious tendencies which I, too, possessed, but which had been suppressed for a long time. The desire to be in touch with the eternal began to assert itself. This soon led me to think of prayer.

I had to admit to myself that the "intellectually" and "scientifically" established view of life which I had adopted had left a peculiar feeling of emptiness within me. This feeling soon began to pass over into restlessness. Now and then I felt an inner anxiety which I could not understand and which was, therefore, the more annoying.

Gradually it dawned on me that I had, after all, pursued a wrong course in thinking that a man could and should live his life without conscious fellowship with God— without religion.

I now said to myself that my inner emptiness is due to the fact that my soul-life lacks the religious element. There is something about religious meditation and especially religious prayer which will fill the great void in my soul. My soul-life will become harmonious and balanced again when I become established in fellowship with God.

I began to pray.

Notice now the attitude I had when I began to pray. In the first place, I did not believe in answer to prayer on God's part. I denied the very possibility of God being able or willing to give any heed to what a capricious individual might happen to ask of Him. I saw in prayer nothing but a purely subjective movement in my soul upward toward the eternal. I had no other effect of prayer in mind than a purely subjective one: that my soul might become concentrated upon God and the eternal. I looked upon that as a sound and profitable diversion from my soul's concentration upon temporal and corruptible things.

In the second place, and in this connection the most important, I did not turn to God to speak candidly and confidentially with Him. It was by no means my intention to cease my worldly and selfish life. On the contrary, my attempt to pray was a semi-conscious or unconscious effort to find peace and rest in order that I might keep up my worldly life, undisturbed by the more or less clear reproaches of my conscience.

That is the reason why I was unsuccessful in prayer. I did not get in touch with God. My prayer was a monologue, a soliloquy. It did not rise to heaven; but was like the smoke from Cain's sacrifice, which lay close to the earth.

My attempt to pray was, accordingly, very brief. The little sincerity that was left in me revolted against a religiosity of this kind, against such fellowship with God.

*

Permit me now to tell you what happened when I really began to pray in such a way that I received an answer and entered into fellowship with the unseen God.

That did not take place until I was in dire need.

It was no longer merely a question of a little inner emptiness or restlessness, or some little outward need or sorrow or reversal from which I desired to be freed through my supplications. Now it was my sin that made me restless. And it finally made me so restless that I did not dare to live in it any longer.

I tried first to break with my sinful habits. I dare say that I made a serious attempt, but I failed completely. The more I saw of my own life, the clearer it became to me that my real sinfulness lay in my self-loving and self-centered heart. It was not long before I had to admit that I was utterly helpless in my struggle.

Then it was that I turned to God in earnest prayer.

I had turned to God before for the sake of a little religious diversion and for relief from the feeling of emptiness and restlessness which annoyed me.

Now I turned to God in order to speak candidly and confidentially with Him. The first thing I said to Him was this: "Lord, speak Thou to me. Speak to me in such a way that I will understand that it is Thou who speakest. Tell me what Thou hast to tell about my life and my heart. I do not come to Thee with the intention of deceiving Thee, but to be reconciled to Thee and to be saved from my sins. Do unto me whatsoever Thou wilt. I have no demands to make upon Thee. I only pray Thee to save me. Use whatever means Thou mayest find necessary."

That is the substance of what I said to Him; the wording may have been slightly different.

And I received an answer.

Not exactly what I had thought beforehand it would be. But from that moment He gripped my soul so powerfully that I could not deny the fact without being untrue to myself.

At first there were many difficulties indeed. Often He did not hear me at all, or the answer was so indistinct that I was not certain of it in my own mind. But from that time nothing could scare me away from Him or cause me to lose courage. Had I not said that He might use whatever means He might find necessary? I had to rest satisfied with what He did, even though I did not always understand His ways with me.

When He delayed answering me, I was impelled more than ever to examine myself diligently before Him, asking myself if there was anything wrong with my life or with my heart which He by this means desired to point out to me.

*

We have now reached the point which is to determine whether you are to remain a doubter or be delivered from skepticism.

The question is simply this: Are you willing to break with your former manner of life or are you not?

If you are unwilling to break with the sinful life you have been living, then put aside every hope of ever being rid of your doubts.

I know, recalling the time when I myself was a doubter, that this seems like a hard saying to you. It is very natural for you to take the view that if you could only rid yourself of your doubts, then you would, as a matter of course, gladly become a new man and lead a new life. Meanwhile, when your conscience condemns you most severely because of your selfish and frivolous life, it may be that you even make use of your inner uncertainty as a shield against the accusations of your conscience. You say to yourself that as long as everything is so uncertain and absolute truth does not exist as far as you are concerned you, of course, have not the power to take a firm stand against sin.

Theoretically this seems absolutely unassailable.

However, I presume that the same thing which happened to me, happened to you also. Your conscience would not be satisfied with such evasiveness. It demanded an unequivocal break with your former manner of life. It insisted, furthermore, that you were not honest when you put the blame upon your doubts. Finally it said: Can you who are not even willing to be truthful expect to stand in the presence of a holy God and have Him help you to overcome your skepticism?

Permit me to underline what your conscience has already told you. There is no other way to salvation than by honestly breaking with sin, the narrow but safe way of repentance. Do not think that God has ordained a separate way of salvation for doubters. No, in this

respect there is no difference. We must all pass through
the narrow gate of repentance if we desire to have fellowship with God.

You recall, no doubt, that on Good Friday Jesus was
sent from Pilate to Herod. Herod was much pleased
at this. For a long time he had been desirous of seeing Him because he hoped to see Jesus perform a
miracle before his eyes. The account of their meeting
closes with these characteristic words: "He questioned
Him in many words; but He answered him nothing"
(Luke 23:9).

The man who turns to Jesus without seeking salvation from his sins receives no answer to his prayers even
if he prays, as Herod did, in many words.

If you are among these, do not go away and say, as
so many do, that Christianity is only imagination and
vain talk; and that you may cry, even cry aloud and
weep in your distress, but receive no reply. Do not allow such cheap talk to mislead you. Give heed to the
plain words of Jesus: "If any man willeth to do His
will, he shall know of the teaching, whether it is of God,
or whether I speak from myself."

From the moment that you turn to Christ for the purpose of making an honest accounting of all your sins and
of being saved from your former manner of life, you
will be answered by your invisible Saviour. Even though
the answer may come in a way somewhat different from
what you had thought, you will, nevertheless, receive the
answer you need. And it will be one which will both
frighten you and beckon to you at the same time.

*

Permit me at this time to repeat my advice to every

honest doubter: Begin to read the New Testament and begin to pray.

Speak candidly and confidentially with God about your daily experience in trying to do the will of God, as I mentioned above. It will lift you up into a natural and unstudied relationship of confidence toward God. You will feel secure and happy as you withdraw from the multitude and from the tumult of life and, having entered into your secret chamber, pour out your heart to God, telling Him of your selfishness, your sins of omission, the sins you have committed, and, worst of all, the insincerity of your attitude toward your fellow men, toward yourself, and even toward God Himself.

You will now have additional new experiences, which will enable you to learn experimentally what the very essence of Christianity is and thus obtain true Christian assurance.

As you read in the New Testament about Christ and live in fellowship with Him, confiding to Him each day the facts concerning your inner as well as your outward life, you will, like all the rest of us, experience that there arises in your heart a singular attitude of confidence toward Him.

He who has seen the sunlight has no need of any one to explain to him that it is light and not darkness. Likewise, he who in prayer enters deeper and deeper into fellowship with Christ as He is given to us in the New Testament has no need of any one to explain to him that he is in fellowship with God. He apprehends here the life, the words, and the mighty acts of the Absolute One.

Confronted with the Absolute, there is only one thing for man to do: submit in unconditional obedience and yield in absolute confidence. That every one knows who in sincere prayer has studied the New Testament testimony of Christ. The confidence which Christ thus wins from us makes it natural for us to rely on what He says. Before, on the other hand, we would have thought that we had been compelled to submit to His sayings, so often paradoxical and incomprehensible.

If we have experienced what Søren Kierkegaard expresses in the words, "before God we are always in the wrong," then we know Christ as our real, true Lord. And to submit to Him does not make us stunted or spineless beings. On the contrary, we experience an inner emancipation to be permitted to submit to Him in unqualified confidence and obedience. The more wholeheartedly and unreservedly we submit to Him, the more we succeed both in finding ourselves and in being ourselves.

*

As already indicated, the fellowship with God which I have described so far is replete with severe struggles. There is not much joy, peace, or assurance. During this period your spiritual life will, as a rule, vacillate strongly between fear and peace, anxiety and joy.

There are times when God is experienced as being so near that your soul leaps with joy. At other times your soul is quiet, dead. You feel nothing and will nothing. It is a peculiarly negative condition, in which you feel almost entirely unconcerned about your relation to God. At other times, again, you feel sick and sore at heart.

It seems to you as though God has forsaken you. Even worse is the fact that you think you yourself are to blame, because of your own unfaithfulness and disobedience.

The remarkable thing now is that the nature of your doubt has changed. You are amazed and can scarcely recognize either yourself or your doubts.

Heretofore, theoretical doubt and mental antagonism toward the Christian faith have been uppermost in your soul. Now, however, you are really not much concerned about intellectual difficulties. Possibly they have not all as yet been solved in your own mind. Nevertheless, they now occupy your thoughts but very little.

As a matter of fact, entirely new problems have arisen, which occupy your soul's entire attention and engage all its strength. The distress of your conscience now completely overshadows the previous distress of your intellect. The distress of your conscience became great when, as I mentioned above, you began to see your selfishness and your sentimental insincerity in excusing and defending your sinfulness instead of confessing it openly both to yourself and to others. Later this distress became even greater.

At first your soul, impelled by great anxiety, devoted itself to fervent prayer and intimate communion with God. The truths of the Bible made a deep impression upon you during this time. Everything was new and fresh. Your soul was like wax. The faintest impression left a clear, distinct mark.

Your former sins, too, had been given a shock, so to speak. The painful distress which you had experienced had left a distaste for the lust and sweetness of sin. For this reason temptations had but little power during this period. Consequently, it was not difficult during this time to retain tranquility of conscience. There was a marked change both in your life and in your heart.

However, as soon as the strong emotions subsided, you began to experience something very different. The desire to sin reasserted itself with redoubled strength. Even though you desisted from carrying it out in word or deed, you saw, nevertheless, that you did not hate sin, but loved it.

During this time you read the New Testament, perhaps every day. But, honest as you now were with yourself, you were compelled to admit that you had no desire to do so. Newspapers interested you a great deal more. You read them with eagerness. You prayed to God also, perhaps every day. But you had to force yourself to do that too.

Others thought well of you. They saw, of course, the great change which had taken place in your life. But the more highly they thought of you, the worse you yourself felt about your own condition. You felt that there was something false and hypocritical about yourself, which pained you almost more than everything else you now were experiencing.

To make matters even worse, you felt cold and indifferent in the midst of it all. To begin with you were deeply grieved because of your terrible spiritual condition. But gradually this sorrow vanished completely, and, instead, you now felt cold, callous, and unconcerned.

The worst of all, however, was that little by little you began to doubt your own sincerity. Never before had you known that you were such a vacillating and fickle character. At times you were much concerned about salvation from sin and from your own insincerity. At other times, again, you felt such a desire toward sin that you would sacrifice nothing for the sake of becoming a new man.

Then when you turned to God each day to receive the forgiveness of sins, you felt that to do so was blasphemy toward a holy God. You asked yourself incessantly if God could forgive a man who secretly loves and clings to the sin for which he was asking pardon. Would it not be a violation of the moral law on the part of God to forgive such a person?

*

My doubting friend, when you have experienced a little of this, you have, in the midst of all your doubt and distress, reached a stronger faith in God than that of which you yourself are fully aware.

Faith begins, as you know, in all of us as faith, first and foremost, in God's holy law, His ethical will. It was so in the case of God's own people, Israel. They had to learn first to believe God's holy law.

Note now, my friend, how you have learned that very thing, by the wisdom and grace of God. You have received direct, personal assurance that what Christ has said to you is the will of God. You have submitted to God's will. You have admitted that its demands upon you are absolute, that you are unconditionally and absolutely under obligation to live according to it. When you observe daily that you do not do it, you feel that you are totally condemned; you even despise and detest yourself. And you consider it out of the question that God will or can have anything to do with you so long as your moral condition is such.

Now begins in earnest that spiritual cry which is common to all who have begun in truth to have fellowship with Christ in prayer and the reading of the New Testament: "How can I find a gracious God? My sin! My sin! How can I secure the forgiveness of sins?"

Note what fellowship with Christ has accomplished in you. Before, the question of the forgiveness of sins was the simplest thing in the world to you. You thought that as soon as you confessed your sins, God would, of course, forgive—and that matter would be all very nicely taken care of. It had often irritated you to see people tormenting themselves with fear and anxiety lest God should not forgive them their sins. They appeared to you to be morbid souls, who had lost the ability to distinguish between essentials and non-essentials.

Now you look upon this matter differently.

Now the question of the forgiveness of sins is the most difficult one you have faced in your whole life. Theoretical and intellectual difficulties have been reduced to mere bagatelles in comparison with the doubt and anxiety which now torment you. You may even smile at times, perhaps, when you recollect that not long ago there was a time in your life when the question of the divinity of Christ, His supernatural birth, and His bodily resurrection were your greatest difficulties.

*

If you have had these experiences, my doubting friend, you are prepared to receive full assurance concerning Christ and His wonderful salvation. Up to this time you have not been prepared.

This is a fact which is frequently overlooked. In our day, especially, it seems as though people have forgotten that there is no other way of becoming personally assured of Christ and of the Christian faith than this: the way of the sinner, the way which leads through complete despair of self.

Christ Himself knew full well that there was something about His person which would be and must needs be an occasion of stumbling. Therefore, too, He said upon one occasion: "Blessed is he whosoever shall find no occasion of stumbling in me" (Matthew 11:6). As early as at the time of His birth the following prophetical words were spoken of Him: "This child is set for the falling and rising of many in Israel" (Luke 2:34).

This was revealed already in the days of His flesh.

Publicans and sinners, who realized their sinfulness, found in Him no occasion of stumbling. In their distress they turned to Him, drawn by the truth which brought them low into the dust, guilty before the face of God, and attracted by the mild and tender love which He showed toward every sincere soul that willingly accepted the sentence of condemnation which the truth decreed.

These publicans and sinners received Him as He was, without criticizing Him or desiring to change Him. There were things about Him, of course, which they did not understand, and which they found might even be occasions of stumbling. But this did not affect their faith in Him.

As soon as they had submitted to the truth of His word and had come to a realization of their complete helplessness, but also by His creative word had been raised up to a new life, with peace in their hearts and a new mind to do the will of God, He became the authority to Whom they submitted in all things and in Whom they confided.

We see, on the other hand, that the religious leaders of the people, the Scribes and the Pharisees, did find occasion of stumbling in Jesus. They criticized Him in many ways. They named very exacting conditions upon which they would recognize Him as the Messiah. They were not satisfied with His personal life, His teachings, or His conduct among the people.

But we see also that these people, with few exceptions, never became concerned about their sins when they heard Jesus preach. The Gospel records show us this very clearly. Jesus Himself has given us His general view of the whole matter in the parable of the Pharisee and the Publican.

Here we are at the deepest root, the first hidden beginnings, of the Christian faith.

Jesus is such that He must be an occasion of stumbling among men. To the ordinary, average person He is unreal and doubtful from first to last, with respect to His divine origin, His supernatural birth, His miraculous works, His vicarious suffering and death, His bodily resurrection, His ascension, and His return to judgment.

This is also the reason why many in our day, as in the time of Christ, go away from Him in indifference and live their lives as though Christ had never lived—just as the large majority of the Jewish people in the time of Jesus did. Others can not go away from Him so easily. Like the scribes and the Pharisees, they keep circling about Him. But they are not satisfied with Him. As He confronts them in the New Testament they will not acknowledge Him as their Saviour.

Some of them, too, have the boldness to tell us openly what changes they must make in Him before they can make use of Him as their Saviour. In the first place, He must not be eternal God. He must not have been conceived and born in a supernatural manner. He must not have performed any miracles; and His suffering and death must have no vicarious significance. Above all He must not be risen from the dead. And faith in such a "Saviour" has been called Christianity!

But this is historical deception, the more reprehensible because it has been perpetrated by men with scientific training. They should know that Christianity is a historic religion, with its own definite historical characteristics. Christianity is an historical fact. And we treat facts scientifically, not by telling what they ought to be, but by showing what they actually are.

Christianity has always been faith in Christ, not a Christ such as the Pharisees and other scribes desired and demanded that He should be, but faith in Christ as preached by the apostles, whose testimony to Christ as contained in the New Testament is acknowledged by all branches of the church as the inspired Word of God and the infallible guide for faith, doctrine, and life.

That is what historic Christianity has been from the beginning and is today.

Yes, they say, but no modern man can believe in such a Christ any longer.

To this the church answers that modern man, highly interesting as He is, is not the only one who has not been able to believe in this Saviour. Exactly the same objection was raised over nineteen hundred years ago: "This is a hard saying, who can hear it?"

The church answers, further, that there have been people in every age who have found occasion of stumbling in Jesus. There is only one possible way for all of them to learn to know Him and to believe on Him as He is given us of God. And that is by becoming convicted of sin. Christ is acceptable and "intelligible" only to publicans and sinners who by Jesus' word of truth have been bowed down into the dust before the living God, who acknowledge that they are completely lost, and who know of nothing else to do but to throw themselves into the open arms of Jesus.

*

Permit me now, after this digression, to return to your experiences, my doubting friend.

I pray you, remember our agreement: I did not take it upon myself to prove to you the truth of Christianity. I promised to point out the experiences through which you would have to pass in order to become personally convinced of the truth of Christianity. I also promised to show you what to do in order to gain these experiences.

I have now followed you step by step into the world of experience which opens itself to you through earnest prayer and the reading of the New Testament. We have now reached the point where you in fellowship with your Saviour have become a helpless sinner, and from the depths of your soul you cry out for full assurance that all sins be forgiven and that you be received into fellowship with God.

Gradually there has grown up within you an attitude of confidence toward Christ which you beforehand had not thought possible. He is now your highest, your absolute, authority. You acknowledge that what He has said is divine truth. You feel that the gentle tenderness and mercy which He bestowed upon the helpless sinners who came to Him is a constant balm and healing to your weary and aching soul.

When you read about this or meditate upon other words of Jesus, you experience an inner composure which refreshes your weary, struggling soul. But you experience this only at brief intervals. You long for an experience such as they had who came to Jesus. He spoke a word to them, a creative word, which lifted them out of their inner distress and restlessness and transformed them into confident and glad disciples.

You surmise that Jesus can and will give you more than you have received. When you read the New Testament and when you read or hear about true Christians down through the history of the Church, you realize that they had more than you have received so far. Not that you are ungrateful for what you have already received. Even though it has so far, in the main, brought you inward distress and spiritual conflict, you would not for the whole world return to your former manner of life. You would not exchange places with those foolish men whose rejoicing is in the things of this world. You would rather sow the seeds of godliness with tears than do that.

You have surmised rightly. You have not as yet experienced the deepest and most mysterious things in Christianity. Your faith is, as is the case with all beginners, essentially a longing, sighing, I might almost say, doubting, faith. Exactly as the man in the Gospels expressed it in his cry of distress to Jesus: "I believe, Lord, help my unbelief!" (Mark 9:24).

This longing faith is now to become, through a new experience on your part, a happy, peaceful, and assured faith.

Permit me at this point to say a few words about the attitude you should take while waiting for this experience. First, it is not for you to force yourself into this assurance. That is the work of the Spirit. As the great apostle upon one occasion expressed it: "The Spirit beareth witness with our spirit that we are the children of God" (Romans 8:16).

You should continue to speak candidly and confidentially with God. Tell Him that you lack that mystical experience of Christ which makes Him a present reality to your soul and thereby imparts to you a deep and abiding assurance. Then ask Him to prepare you outwardly and inwardly in such a way that you may as soon as possible be ready for this experience. Ask Him each day to direct your attention to everything in your life which either directly or indirectly might hinder the Spirit from making you a partaker in the whole fulness of salvation.

Search yourself daily before God. Pray often the deep and fruitful prayer of the psalmist: "Search me, O God, and know my heart: Try me, and know my thoughts; And see if there be any wicked way in me, And lead me in the way everlasting" (Psalm 139:23-24).

Then, too, you should diligently use the Word of God, whether it appeals to you or not. Whether you think it helps you or not. Before you open your Bible, pray humbly that the Spirit of God may make the Word helpful to you, even though you may not always be certain at the time as to how it is helping you.

Remember the words of Jesus: "Sanctify them in the truth: thy word is truth" (John 17:17). Every time you come in contact with the saving truths of Scripture, a sanctifying influence is imparted to your soul. You are lifted into a different spiritual atmosphere, which is healthful and strengthening to your inner life even though you can not always tell just when a truth has gripped your soul and taken captive your thought.

In the next place, I advise you to participate in the Lord's Supper.

At this point I am prepared to hear you raise an objection again. You say: "I do not understand the Lord's Supper, and that would undoubtedly disturb me during the communion hour. In all likelihood I do not have the right conception of the Lord's Supper either. Perhaps my ideas concerning it are entirely wrong. Is it right to go to the Lord's Supper when I am in this condition? Should I not wait until these things become clearer to me?"

No, you should not. You have a spiritual right to attend the Lord's Supper if you are a sincere disciple of Jesus, that is, one who would conceal no sin from Him but openly confesses to Him everything that troubles your conscience, one who trusts in Jesus and is assured that what He did and said is right, also in that which He said and did when He instituted the Lord's Supper.

You do not understand the Lord's Supper; you are afraid that your conception of it is not right. But Jesus has never demanded of us that we must understand either Him or His Supper. He says rather: "Believe in God, believe also in Me" (John 14:1). Tell Him that you are afraid that you do not have the right ideas about the Lord's Supper. Ask Him, too, to give you the right conception of it as far as it is possible for us human beings to think correctly concerning these high and holy things.

But, above all, remember that it is not a question of your conception of the Lord's Supper. The important thing here is your confidence in Christ and your obedience to Him.

According to Jesus' own words, you are to do this in remembrance of Him.

What are you to do? That which Jesus Himself asks you to do at the communion table: "Take, eat! this is My body, which is given for you" as He says concerning the bread. And concerning the cup He says: "Drink ye all of it, for this is My blood which is poured out for you unto the remission of sins."

If you will do this in obedient confidence toward Christ, you will receive the invisible gift which He once for all has attached to this mysterious act. Even if your conception of the Supper should be correct, that would not make the gift which you receive any greater. And if your conception should be incorrect, that would not lessen the gift which you receive, if you bow in humble submission to Jesus' own words and His own holy ordinance.

Finally, I would advise you to seek the fellowship of people who, you are convinced, live wholeheartedly with Christ.

All religions create fellowships. Christianity does so in a special sense. Christ desires to bind together His disciples into a holy brotherhood of the finest and most intimate kind. The followers of Jesus have understood this. From the beginning they have banded themselves together into the communion of saints, in which they share with each other the mutual blessings which they possess in their common Saviour. They meet regularly to read and speak of Him, to pray and give thanks to Him, and to praise Him.

Seek out the church of God and participate in its life and work.

I know very well that you will be inclined to look upon the secret chamber as the only real place for intimate communion with God. But remember that the Christian's life should not, like the mystic's, rotate about one point, the secret chamber. The Christian's life should rather be like an ellipse, which revolves about two fixed points: the secret chamber and the communion of saints. Our inner life with God will suffer to the extent that we neglect these two centers of Christian edification.

In this connection let me give you a more special bit of advice. Seek out one or two Christians to whom you can confidentially open your heart and with whom you can share everything. Pray God that you may find such Christian friends. You will soon learn how important it is for the weak, unstable new life within you to be permitted to live and to grow in fellowship with some one who has perhaps progressed a little farther than you. To be permitted to exchange thoughts and discuss your experiences in that new life which you have in common, will not only mean spiritual enrichment to both of you, but will also be a help to you against temptation, especially when you are tempted to discouragement and despair.

*

In conclusion permit me to mention the last, the decisive experience, that which leads to Christian assurance in its fulness.

Some fair day, or perhaps some dark night, the miracle will take place in you as it has in millions before you, unexpectedly and, as a rule, suddenly. As a rule it will be a brief passage of Scripture which will become "living" to your soul. As through a little window you will look through this passage into the world of invisible things. Everything will be clear to your inner eye. You will see the Saviour, the cross, and God's eternal love in an entirely new light.

All your doubts and difficulties will be swept away. You will see now what you have in your Saviour. All your sins and the wickedness of your heart will be lost in the boundless depths of grace. They will be like sparks from the funnel of a steamer as they fall into the great ocean. You will be certain that your sins are forgiven, that you are loved of God, that you are His child.

All will be as clear as daylight to you. You will not be able to understand how you could have lived so long without being able to grasp the simple truth that Christ stepped into your place, atoned for all your sins, and made you free.

You have now received assurance, an assurance of

which you could not have dreamed before. Now all the doubters and blasphemers and infidels in the world could come, if they wanted to, and stand in array before you with all their doubts and misgivings. They would not move you a hair's breadth. You would only be glad of the opportunity to speak this personal word to them: "You may doubt, blaspheme, and deny as long as you wish. I possess an assurance which is unknown to you. And if you knew it, you would never again say a word against the assurance which the Christians possess. You would rather begin to pray God that you also might experience it. Yea, you would sacrifice everything in order to gain it."

Having had this experience, you will wonder especially at one or two things.

First, that it was the cross which gave you the assurance. You could never have dreamed of that before. Up to this time the cross had been the most perplexing thing in Christianity. Like many others before you, you thought that the cross was the very thing in Christianity which made Christianity doubtful and was the reason for your skepticism. For that reason you, too, had joined the chorus of modernists who demand that the message of the cross be cut away and that Christianity be presented to the modern mind in a form which can draw men to Christ and not drive them away from Him.

And now it is your experience that it was the cross which brought to your soul the final solution and opened to you all the glories of the kingdom of heaven.

Now no one needs to tell you that the cross is the great heart of Christianity. Now you see that the cross shines forth from every page of the New Testament. And now you understand why the greatest of all the apostles, wher ever he went, even in the world's greatest centers of culture, proclaimed nothing else save the cross. He himself expressed it thus: "And I, brethren, when I came unto you, came not with excellency of speech or of wisdom, proclaiming to you the testimony of God. For I determined not to know anything among you, save Jesus Christ, and Him crucified" (1 Corinthians 2:1-2).

You now begin to realize what an unholy crime all the modern religious quacks are perpetrating who remove the stumblingblock of the cross from Christianity in order to give it a greater appeal to modern man. The great apostle has expressed himself also in regard to this with all the clearness one could wish for: "For the word of the cross is to them that perish foolishness, but unto us who are saved it is the power of God. . . . But we preach Christ crucified, unto Jews a stumblingblock, and unto Gentiles foolishness" (1 Corinthians 1:18, 23).

The other thing which will cause you to wonder after you have had this experience is that your assurance with regard to the cross and the Crucified One is not based upon a mental solution of the mystery of the cross. Christ's vicarious suffering and death is still an impenetrable mystery to your intellect. The remarkable thing now is that the unintelligible aspect of the cross no longer causes you any intellectual distress. Consequently, it is no longer a source of doubt.

You possess an assurance which is more fundamental than all logic. You have experienced the cross and now have the direct assurance of experience, which is independent of your intellectual ability to reason out your experience.

*

Permit me to add a few words concerning this experience, not in order to explain it, but to emphasize that it is not something which you are to press out from within yourself by means of auto-suggestion or other psychological hyper-tension.

You should not attempt to do anything aside from that which I have advised you to do in the preceding, namely, to make diligent use of the means of grace which Christ has given us, praying each day that you may become a partaker in the full assurance of salvation. At the psychological moment the Spirit will accomplish the miracle within you which will impart to you the assurance described above.

The miracle consists in this, that He opens to you the invisible, eternal world in a new way. It is the work of the Spirit in the dispensation of salvation to establish contact between the eternal and the temporal world, between visible and invisible reality.

This He does by giving the truly repentant sinner that new spiritual sight which "sees" the invisible reality, that new spiritual sense which is capable of functioning in the realm of the eternal. You experience Christ and the realm of grace and salvation of which He is the central figure in a direct, intuitive way. You experience Him as a present, blessed reality. In the moment that you with your new spiritual senses apprehend the invisible world of grace in which the cross is the center, in that moment a new life dawns upon your whole inner and outward being.

You see your relation to God from the perspective of eternity. You now see what the cross of Christ and the death of Christ mean to you. You now see what it means to be "in Christ." You now experience with all your new spiritual senses what it means to be a child of God by grace alone. Your soul is filled with unspeakable joy and with that peace which "passeth all understanding" (Philippians 4:7).

At the same time your attitude toward outward things, toward men and toward the rest of the world about you, has also changed. You have been given grace to look at everything in the light of eternity. And, looking upon your fellow men in this light, you look upon them no longer as individuals who by mere chance happen to cross your path in various ways, nor as people who are a little more or a little less pleasing; you look first and last toward that within them which is eternal and immortal.

That gives you, in the first place, a deep respect for them. In the second place, you become earnestly concerned about these souls who, as a rule, busy themselves during their brief span of life with destroying both themselves and others. In other words, you have begun to look upon life as Jesus did. That means that you go with Him into the work of saving them.

The world of things, too, appears different to your eye when you view it in the clear light of eternity. You will be surprised at the new appraisal of values which you will make as you come in touch again with old, familiar things. You will find that things which you formerly deemed indispensable, no longer mean much to you. In fact, you will feel that some of them are unquestionably dangerous to the new life within you. And therefore you are determined to part with them.

You will have such experiences in connection with your reading, your associations, and your pleasures. From the depths of your heart you will subscribe to the words of the apostle: "Wherefore if any man is in Christ, he is a new creature: the old things are passed away; behold, they are become new" (II Corinthians 5:17).

Are all your doubts and difficulties now solved?

No, likely not. But you have experienced what Jesus promised you : you know that the teaching is of God. The statements of the Bible concerning Christ have become the Word of God to you. Through this Word He has spoken to you in such a way that you are certain that it is God who has spoken.

You have experienced this word as the transforming Word of God, which first changed you from a frivolous to a despairing sinner, who had no peace in sin but had to turn to the living God for salvation, and then transformed you from a despairing sinner to a non-doubting, free, and saved sinner.

This has given you a faith in the Bible which enables you freely and gladly to live and to die by it. The Bible has become the authority to which you submit in all things pertaining to salvation, and according to which you feel safe in living your life.

To be sure, you may still come upon passages in the Bible which give you trouble. The human side of the Scriptures, especially, may give you much intellectual difficulty, as you try to co-ordinate in your mind the divine and the human sides of the Biblical word.

But these intellectual difficulties will not cause you the distress that they did before. Your new experiences have helped you. Now you say to yourself that since I have experienced assurance with regard to the vital point, namely, that God has met me in Christ and raised me up to a new, rich, and blessed life, I expect also to receive assurance with respect to the other things about which I still feel uneasy and uncertain. Since I have had the greatest of all intellectual crosses, the cross of Christ, transformed into a source of happy assurance to me, why should I then worry about the lesser intellectual crosses?

Here, too, I have a bit of advice to offer you.

In the first place, be honest with yourself. Do not try to conceal from yourself the fact that you are still uncertain and in doubt on these points. Acknowledge it openly to yourself. Above all, speak with God about it in prayer. Ask Him to give you experimental assurance also with respect to these things, thus solving your mental difficulties and giving you direct assurance.

In the second place, be patient! Take time!

Let God quietly prepare you for and give you those experiences which will dispel also these doubts. And while you are waiting, do not permit yourself to become anxious about these things. Just tell God that they trouble you, and that you are longing for inner peace and rest also with regard to these points.

In the third place, while waiting for this assurance and struggling with these doubts, do not permit yourself to yield to the temptation of denying any part of that which the Christian church has believed and confessed from the beginning.

Confess openly that you do not have personal assurance with regard to certain articles of the Christian faith. But say also that you are in all humility longing and praying that you may share the Christian church's apostolic faith at every point and that you are looking forward with rejoicing to the day when, together with the living church of God, you can freely confess every article of the Christian faith.

BOOK THREE

Why I Am a Christian

MY THEME might also have been formulated thus: Why I became a Christian. For I had lived for many years as a religious heathen. At that time, too, I naturally had my own ideas about the Christians and about their reasons for becoming Christians. Most of them, it seemed to me, became Christians out of fear. They were afraid of divine punishment, of everlasting torment especially. Others, it appeared to me, were less afraid, but were wiser. They wanted to fare well, preferably both here and in the hereafter.

But whether they were afraid or they were wise, or both, it seemed to me that they looked upon Christianity as the safest and at the same time the cheapest kind of insurance, offering benefits which extended even beyond death and the grave.

Now I think differently with regard to this.

It happens, you know, that we must revise our opinions, especially after we have had personal experience with a thing and not merely thought or speculated about it.

I have had personal experience in this matter. And if I were to tell you why I became a Christian and were to give my answer quickly and in one short sentence, I think that I would have to state it thus, to be as simple and as clear as possible: I did it to become a man.

This may perhaps sound somewhat strange to some people. But I know of no task which is so great and so difficult as that of becoming a man.

I know of statesmen who have rendered such great services to their country that their names are taught to and admired by every school child. I know of scientists who have done so much for humanity that their names will be mentioned to the end of time. I know of artists whose fame has spread throughout the whole civilized world. But many of these live their real lives, that which men thoughtlessly and superficially refer to as their private lives, in such a way that it is usually omitted from their biographies.

To be a real artist, a scientist, or a statesman requires certain definite abilities and training, but to be a real man requires not a little more than both ability and training. We have schools for educating men to become farmers, craftsmen, business men, professional men, and for training them for many other vocations in life; but whether these schools help to make men of these people or not, I am not so certain. Neither do I know, as far as that is concerned, whether a school which sought only to make men out of people would have a very large attendance.

*

As I look around in this remarkable world in which I find myself, I soon discover that all life is subject to its own particular laws. Among these laws I find, again, two which are fundamental and which recur in all forms of life.

In the first place, all life, in plants, in animals, in fish, and in man, has a nature which is peculiar to itself. If we sow oats, we reap oats, not barley. From birds' eggs we get birds, not fish.

In the second place, every form of life, each with its own peculiar characteristics, is dependent upon certain outward conditions. Some plants must have sunlight; others, shade. Some animals must have water in which to live; others, air; others, earth; and still others must be below the earth's surface.

If they are not allowed to live in these particular surroundings, the result will be an impaired life, ending finally in death. Think of a bird in a cage, or of a bear in captivity. Have you ever seen an evergreen, the tallest tree in our forests, standing in a swamp? It is short, moss-covered, and full of dry branches. No one would think that it was the queen of our forests.

Man, too, is subject to certain laws.

Human life has its own peculiar characteristics, which make it human. And this life develops only under certain conditions and in certain environments.

One of the characteristics of human life, among others, is that it must discover its own peculiarity, that is, discover the meaning of life. In all other living beings the innate life unfolds itself automatically, by means of the instincts. In man, however, the unfolding of life takes place consciously and deliberately.

Man himself must know what it means to be a man, and will to be it. He himself must select the environment in which his own peculiar life can unfold itself. And this is what men have been working at down through the ages as far back as we have any historical records of human life. The best men and women of each generation have been the ones who have sacrificed the most time and energy to ascertain the meaning of life.

One day a quiet, good man came forth and said: "I have found it."

Men crowded around him and listened. After they had heard him to the end, they said: "Verily, we have found it!"

And a religion had been founded upon earth.

Now, all life is supplied with a peculiar apparatus which we call sensitiveness or feeling. It constitutes a very important factor in life. It serves life both positively and negatively. It serves positively by making the living organism aware of those things or conditions which will promote its existence. Even in plants we can clearly discern a "sensitiveness" of this kind. If a tree, for instance, is growing in lean earth and there is better earth a short distance away, we notice that the tree practically moves away from the lean earth by sending its roots over into the good earth.

The feelings serve the living organism negatively by making it aware of everything in its surroundings which is detrimental to its existence. Thus, for instance, the sensitiveness of our skin. It helps us to protect our bodies against dangerous cold or heat. If we touch a hot iron, our feelings give instant warning and we withdraw our hand, thereby escaping greater injury.

This is so self-evident that we think little of it. One of my old friends, however, told me that he lost the sense of feeling in one of his hands as the result of a stroke and that he no longer feels any pain when he burns himself. As a result his hand might now easily be badly injured by terrible burns.

We see this trait with exceptional clearness in animals. Think of how difficult it is to get a rat or a fox to eat poison. Their sensitiveness intuitively protects the living organism by giving the warning that this is dangerous. This is why wild animals do not eat things that are harmful to them. They pass such things by instinctively. On the other hand, we often notice that domestic animals will eat things which are injurious and destructive to them. By living together with us human beings they have lost some of that sure instinctiveness which they had in their wild state.

Our soul-life, too, has its apparatus for feeling, the function of which is to serve this life by pointing out those things in our environment which are conducive to the well being of the soul and by warning against those things which are detrimental to it. This apparatus of the soul we usually call the conscience. It is a part of that life which is peculiar to man, and a very important part, because it is the life-preserving and life-protecting function of the soul.

Its task is to prove all things both from without and within which affect our spiritual life and to determine whether they are beneficial or detrimental to the soul. If the conscience is permitted to function normally, nothing reaches the soul before the conscience has expressed its opinion concerning it.

When the quiet, good man had spoken, and men had heard from him what the meaning of life was, conscience immediately began its work. It proved all things. But gradually the number of those grew greater and greater who said to themselves and later to others also: this is not the meaning of life.

And they began anew to try to find the answer to the old problem.

One day another man came forth. He, too, was a quiet and a good man. He, too, said: "I have found it."

And people listened and said: "In truth, now we have found it."

And another new religion had been founded on earth.

Thus it continued through hundreds and thousands of years. But the conscience of man was not satisfied with any of the solutions.

*

Then came Jesus.

He showed us what the meaning of life is. When Jesus came, we saw for the first time on earth what a real man is. He called himself the *"Son of Man."*

The others, who had preceded Jesus, could only tell us how a man should be. Jesus, however, exemplified it in His own life. He did not only point out the ideal, as others had done; He Himself was the ideal, and He actually lived it out before our very eyes.

Permit me to mention two things in connection with this ideal. In the first place, Jesus, too, directs His appeal to our consciences. Furthermore, He seeks no other following but that which the consciences of men will grant Him.

Many think that Jesus forces men to follow Him. In so doing they reveal how little they know about Him.

Let me call your attention to one incident in the life of Jesus. It was during the great awakening in Galilee. The people were streaming together and almost trampling one another down. One day Jesus stopped and looked at all these people. And He seemed to ask Himself this question: I wonder if they have understood me? Then He turned and cried out once again to the multitudes: "No man can be my disciple without renouncing all that he hath, yea, even his own life" (Luke 14:25-33).

A man who speaks to the people in that way does not expect to gain any other adherents but such as are convinced in their hearts that both the man and his message are trustworthy and that they, therefore, are inwardly bound to follow him, regardless of what it may cost them.

This is the remarkable thing that happens. When our consciences are confronted by Jesus, we are compelled to accord Him our full and unqualified approval. At least, He received the approval of my conscience. No matter in what situation I see Jesus, my conscience says: Verily, that is the way a man should be.

Whether I see Him as a child or as an adult, in the quiet home circle or in public life, among friends or among enemies, at rest or at work, in conflict, in temptation, in pain, yea, even in death—everywhere, my conscience says: that is the way a man should be.

In the second place, the Jesus-ideal is lofty enough for even the most gifted of men.

Down through the ages there have been many who have thought that they could improve upon the Jesus-ideal. But as yet no one has even been able to approach Him, not to speak of surpassing Him.

Those who have followed Him the farthest have gradually come to such a strong realization of their spiritual inferiority to Him that they have felt themselves unworthy to suffer martyrdom in the same way as He. Thus tradition says that Peter asked to be crucified with his head down because he felt that he was unworthy to hang upon a cross in the same way as his Master.

So high is the goal which Jesus has set for men by His own life. Yet the life which He lived is not beyond any one of us, not even the least gifted. Jesus expressed Himself with regard to this upon one occasion in the following manner: "I thank Thee, O Father, Lord of heaven and earth, that Thou didst hide these things from the wise and the understanding, and didst reveal them unto babes!"

High enough for the most gifted, and yet not beyond the least gifted! In this, too, we see the Master.

*

What, then, was the life of Jesus like?

Large volumes, both scientific and devotional, have, of course, been written about this. I must be brief and shall, therefore, mention only a couple of the fundamental traits, the two which, to my mind, most clearly distinguish the life of Jesus from that of all other people.

In the first place, Jesus never had to grope His way to find the meaning of life, as everybody else has had to do, both before and after His time. Unerringly He discerned it and lived in harmony with it, to Him a perfectly natural way of living. We can not discover that He was ever in doubt, not even during His temptation or His passion.

The unique thing about Jesus, however, that which impresses us most, was, without comparison, His intimate and unbroken fellowship with the Father. He Himself knew that this was the secret of His life, of its radiant purity, as well as its quiet joy and its superhuman power.

He saw immediately and intuitively which were the right relationships in life and which was the proper environment for human life. Consequently His life was that perfectly successful and normal human life which it was. His whole life was rooted in God. He was its vital element. Jesus felt that His meat was to do the will of the Father. He tells us upon one occasion that He never did anything without first "seeing" His Father do it. He never said a word without first "hearing" it of His Father.

He walked upon earth; but lived in heaven, not as a religious dreamer, but as the most practical, the most capable, and the most willing to suffer of all men known to history.

In the second place, I would mention the life Jesus lived among men.

The unique thing about this aspect of His life, as contrasted with our lives, was that He sought the welfare of others to such an extent that He was oblivious of Himself if only He might do some good to others.

Jesus has had many enemies, both among His contemporaries and since, and they have scrutinized His life very closely. None of them, however, has been able to point to a single instance in which Jesus acted from selfish motives.

Jesus has given expression to this normal human life by saying: "Thou shalt love the Lord thy God above all else, and thy neighbor as thyself."

But before speaking about this life to others, He Himself lived it, among friends as well as among His enemies.

*

When I first was given to "see" this picture of Jesus, I had been studying theology for five years. I had passed through all the various stages of doubt. I had doubted the inspiration of the Bible and everything supernatural and miraculous which the Scriptures and the Church had attributed to this Man.

I soon became acquainted with the methods of liberal theology and learned how to employ them. And when I had applied the current religio-historical tests to the little brochures about Jesus written by the four evangelists, there was not a great deal left in them of "scientific" value.

However, this portrait of Jesus can not be destroyed by doubt or by criticism of any kind. It is imprinted upon the four Gospels of our New Testament. And it does its God-given work even when men try, as I did, by means of "science" to tear it to shreds.

During my whole student life I had taken a theoretical and impersonal attitude toward this portrait of Jesus. When I finally did give Christ access to the place which He had always desired to reach, namely my conscience, an entirely new movement was started in my whole inner being.

Permit me at this point to mention the two things which came to mean most to me.

In the first place, concerning the life of Jesus with which I had now come in contact, my conscience compelled me to say: Verily, that is the way a man should be. I began to feel also that the life of Jesus was a condemnation of my own life. I could not help but feel that my life was shameful; it grieved me; and I practically abhorred myself. I felt that my own life was a downright inhuman life.

Some may perhaps think that I had lived an unusually wicked life and had become one of Garborg's "tired men." But such was not the case. A good home and a number of good friends had saved me from a wild life during my youth.

Nevertheless, I now saw how inhuman the life was which I had been living. Jesus lived His life for others. I had lived my whole life for myself, in petty selfishness, pride, and pleasure.

That there were many others even among the theological students who lived as I did, did not help me any longer. My conscience was speaking to me now.

In the second place, the life of Jesus attracted me with a power which I had never before felt in all my life.

I saw before my eyes that pure, good, beautiful, and strong life which God had intended that I should live. It attracted me with a wonderful power.

I could understand now why so many young men were drawn to Jesus. All He had to say to them was: "Follow me," and they left all and followed Him, that wonderful peripatetic teacher.

I was, of course, tempted to continue to live as before; that would naturally have been the easiest and would have involved the least effort. But I felt an indescribable fear at the mere thought of it, because I knew that by so doing I would betray my very innermost self.

Jesus once said: "Every one that is of the truth heareth my voice." Now I knew that Jesus was right. Every one who is confronted by Jesus and refuses to accept Him is untrue to himself.

I had formerly believed that people who became Christians had to deny their own convictions, if they were people who did their own thinking, but now I saw that I had to become a Christian if I was not to be untrue to myself and my most sacred convictions.

Then came the choice.

I had to choose. Do not misunderstand me. I was not compelled to become a Christian. I could choose whichever way I would. That was the terrible thing about it. But I had to choose.

I was to say a few words about why I became a Christian.

I can answer more readily now. I could not endure being untrue to myself, both for time and for eternity. I could not enter upon a life of unequivocal falsehood, such as would have been the case if, after having been confronted with Jesus, I had continued to live as before.

So I chose to follow Jesus.

And God be praised now and forever for that choice! When I had made it, a quiet, peaceful joy descended upon my soul, a joy which I had not known since I was a child. I had made the greatest choice of my life, and my conscience was fully and completely in accord with it.

I had made a whole-hearted decision to follow Jesus.

But you might as well have asked me to climb to the moon as to follow Jesus. The one was as impossible as the other. All day long my conscience would say to me: "Jesus would have done this, but you didn't. Jesus would not have done that, but you did."

Now and then I thought that I really had done what Jesus would have done. Then my conscience would say: "Very well, and everything would be all right if you only had done it in the same spirit as Jesus!"

My despair at this I shall not endeavor to describe. I could not go back to my former way of living. It was impossible to go ahead. Every way was closed.

I began to feel the truth of Jesus' words: "Ye . . . being evil." Before, this hard saying had irritated me more than most of Jesus' sayings. Now, it was beginning to dawn upon me that the great difference between Jesus and us is His spirit. I now began to realize that it was my spirit which made it impossible for me to follow Jesus.

My spirit was one of selfishness throughout. I had myself in mind whether I did good or evil. My own advantage, my own pleasure, my own comfort, or my own honor was always in the background of even the most praiseworthy things I did.

And I could not change my own attitude, even though I was able to change my words and my deeds, which made men believe that a great change had taken place within me. I remember in this connection what one of my friends upon one occasion said to my father about me: "He has become so holy that it is almost too much of a good thing." But I, who knew the condition of my own mind, knew how helplessly unholy I really was.

I was completely at a loss as to what to do.

There I was, under a steady downpour of reproaches from my conscience. The feeling of guilt lay heavily and painfully upon my soul. The desire for forgiveness, for the remission of sins, now became stronger. The human heart's age-old cry after a gracious God began to be heard above all the other voices in my soul.

Scripture speaks about "that which is lost," about the poor, the helpless, those who weep and mourn, who hunger and thirst after righteousness. I had had a feeling before that these expressions were exaggerations, were unnatural, yes, even untruthful and inhuman.

Now, however, they all seemed appropriate, as though they had been written with me in mind. I felt how true everything is which Scripture says concerning man's moral impotence and complete helplessness before God and God's holy, immutable law.

I was now in the dust before the living God. My conscience had brought me to this as I was confronted with the living God and His absolute truth in Jesus Christ. The same thing had happened to me as that which Paul speaks of when he says that his mouth had been stopped and he felt guilty before God.

Now I permitted God to speak to me.

In Jesus Christ I had experienced the absolute God. And when a person is confronted with the Absolute One, he must do one of two things: either reject Him, or cast himself down into the dust before Him. Face to face with the Absolute One, it will not do to bargain, negotiate, or criticize. All such things are silenced when we are confronted with the living God in Jesus Christ.

Søren Kierkegaard has given classic expression to this feeling in the words: "Before God we are always in the wrong." That means that God is always in the right. That is essentially how we feel the authority of God as we stand before Him. Because I have met the living God in Christ, therefore Christ has become my authority, to whom I submit with my deepest and most sacred convictions. I do so voluntarily, and feel secure in so doing.

Jesus Christ had become my Lord, whom I no longer criticized or sought to instruct in religious and moral questions, and to whom I submitted unconditionally whether He spoke about God or man, sin or grace, fall or redemption, heaven or hell, angels or devils, baptism or communion, eternal life or eternal death.

*

I was now in a position to see a new aspect of this most remarkable of all men. I saw that Jesus Himself considered it His real mission to be a Saviour. He was, indeed, our example, our ideal. But He never says that this was the reason for His coming to our world. On the contrary, He said expressly upon various occasions that He came "to give his life a ransom," "to save that which is lost," and that His "blood is poured out unto the remission of sins."

When my eyes were finally opened to this, I saw, of course, that the whole Bible is full of similar truths concerning the Saviour. Why had I not seen this before?

And now I saw, especially in the Gospels, how people whose condition was identical with mine were helped by

Jesus. They were just as oppressed and terrified by their sins as I was. Nevertheless Jesus received them mercifully unto Himself. In fact, I now saw that this was really the thing with which Jesus was constantly occupied.

One thing I noticed especially, namely, the wonderful power in the words of Jesus. He did not merely give good advice, like the founders of other religions had done. When He spoke to a person who in distress had sought Him out, His words took effect immediately and demonstrated their regenerative power.

The people who entered into fellowship with Jesus became new people. If He said to them: "Thy sins are forgiven," they believed His word and became happy, believing souls. If He said: "Follow me," they received power to live a new life in fellowship with Him. I began to understand that there was something about Jesus, about His words and also about His person, which delivered people from their old life, from both the guilt and the power of sin.

In my own mind I often thought: would that I could have lived at the same time as Jesus did! Then I, too, could have received some of that wonderful power which emanated from His mighty person, and my aching and weary soul could have heard at least one single regenerative word from His lips.

*

Then I came in touch with the holy church of God on earth. Or, more correctly, I began to see and to hear what it had been trying to show me and tell me all the time.

There stood the church of God, a never-ending succession of men and women all the way from the morning of Christ's resurrection down to our day. I had, of course, read a great deal about them; and I knew that they were the best men and women that the human race had produced.

There they all stood, saying to me: "We have seen Jesus. He has made us new creatures by His mighty person and His regenerative word. You may see Him, even though He is invisible. Turn to Him in your distress, and you will experience the salvation for which you are so earnestly praying. Go to Him in prayer and study His word intently, and He will reveal Himself to your soul."

I did so, and I very soon experienced a distinct peace. I noticed it especially when I read of the quiet, powerful love which Jesus showed toward all the helpless. I noticed also that the words of Jesus concerning His suffering and death were the ones which gave my soul the greatest security and peace.

I alternated thus for awhile between fear and joy until one day when I experienced the great miracle. In a manner which I can not explain, the mystery of the Gospel, the cross, was unveiled to me. Not in such a way that I could understand it or explain it. I experienced it. Face to face with the crucified Saviour I experienced the God of grace. And that in such a way that all doubt and fear vanished. A happy feeling of security, a blessed assurance, filled my soul, not only for occasional moments, but as an abiding and basic sentiment in my soul.

This would, of course, be dimmed occasionally through spiritual neglect and, especially, through disobedience. But it would return with equal certainty as soon as I sincerely repented at the feet of my Saviour.

*

I now experienced the second great miracle, that which the Bible calls *the new birth*.

An entirely new world was opened to me. Quietly and wondrously I was lifted into the presence of God. As though I had been endowed with a sixth sense, I felt the world of invisible things which surrounded me.

I see now that this invisible world had surrounded me before also. But I lacked the faculties with which to apprehend it and to participate in its life. Now, on the other hand, the eyes of my soul are open; I see the invisible. The ears of my soul are open; I hear the music of heaven. Celestial melodies in mighty billows of rejoicing surge through me, body and soul.

My soul experiences wonderful healing in its new environment. Enveloped by the infinite goodness of God and permeated through and through with that unspeakable peace which the intimate nearness of the Lord imparts, my former life of selfishness loses its attractiveness. By beholding the glory and listening to the music of the invisible and eternal world, my former life with its love of pleasure, honor, and advantage loses its enticing and bewitching power.

Now I know the love of God, but no longer as a heavy and burdensome duty. Now I know the joy of being loved of God for Jesus's sake, and I feel grateful for the privilege of loving Him in return.

I feel that a new moral power is being imparted to my soul. I have come under the personal influence of the mightiest and purest Person in the universe. From Him I am now receiving vital, personal impulses each day. His love it is which gives these impulses their unique power.

I am weighed down when I do anything which grieves my Saviour. I rejoice when I do that which I know is according to His will.

Do not misunderstand me!

I am not sinless or perfect. I often leave the narrow pathway and slip back into my old ways of living, into a self-loving and self-guided life.

But now I know what to do. I tell it all to my Saviour. He leads me back to the right path again. First He forgives me for my unfaithfulness and disobedience and then He works in me both to will and to do according to His good pleasure.

My progress is slow. But I know that the miracle has taken place within me and that Jesus's own life has been planted into my heart.

*

And I find that this new life which I am experiencing is a truly human life, the life for which I was created. I receive direct assurance of this through the inner emancipation which I feel that this life imparts to my whole being.

The more I give myself to this intimate fellowship with my invisible Saviour, the more my soul is filled with that bliss which tells me that I am in my true element and that I am following that plan of life for which I was created. And the more whole-heartedly and frequently I say no to the self-loving and self-directed impulses of my own will, the more I feel that my real human self is being allowed to unfold itself. The more I submit my will to God's will, which is holy love, the unconditional giving of self for others, the more I feel that I find myself and am myself.

Fish are made to live in water. They are free only in water. Birds are made for the air. They are free only in air. I was created to live in God. And I am free only when I am dependent upon Him.

Moreover, I know that He who has begun the good work within me will Himself perfect it. He will not give me up until He has brought me to the goal: to live the same life as He, to love Him above all else and my neighbor as myself.

Then shall I have become what I was created to be: a man.

*

A little incident in closing.

Once earlier during my theological course I had stepped into Professor Petersen's study to get a certificate from him to show that I had completed his course of lectures.

He was known as a man with a lively, jovial nature, who was always master of the situation and knew full well what he wanted. When I asked for the certificate, he assumed a jovial but very astonished mien and inquired: "Why, are you studying theology?"

"Yes," I replied, with all the modesty I could command at the time, "I have ventured to do so."

"And you have not consulted me as yet as to how you should plan your course?"

No, I had not. In parenthesis it might be remarked that Professor Petersen's conservative and warm-hearted Christianity had appealed very little to me during my whole theological course.

"Then I would advise you to make an appointment with me," said the kind old man with a twinkle in his eye.

I promised to do so, and a few days later I sat in Professor Petersen's spacious study in Uranienborg Terrace. I had come to receive his advice.

Meanwhile, the wise old gentleman, who was well acquainted both with me and my theological views, understood very well that I would scarcely profit very much by his advice. Nor was it for the purpose of giving such advice that he had given the hint that I should have a conference with him.

In the course of a half minute or so he had made an end of his counselling. Then he turned and looked me straight in the eye with his own warm, tender eyes and said, after a very brief pause: "Will you not become a Christian, Hallesby?"

Those words and that moment I shall never forget, no matter how old I become.

Like lightning the thought flashed through me: It is true, I am a heathen! That day I received a mortal wound, which within a half year brought me to my knees before my crucified Saviour.

At the time I sought bravely to parry off the well-aimed blow. I summoned to the occasion all my doubts and intellectual difficulties. He listened quietly and patiently to everything I had with which to defend myself. I believe, too, that he answered some of the objections I raised against the intellectual crosses in the Christian faith. My recollection of that, however, is no longer very definite.

Then he suddenly broke off the whole conversation with these words: "Why force this? It will come; it will come!"

My young friends! Today I would send this question along to you. I would ask each one of you: Will you not become a Christian now?

I have now told you a little about why I became a Christian. When in my thoughts I dwell upon the incalculable and unspeakable riches which have been showered upon me since I became a Christian, my desire is that each one of you might also become a Christian.

BOOK FOUR

The Mysterious Element in Christianity

ALL LIFE contains something which our mind is unable to penetrate. We usually term this the mysterious element in life, although we are unable to accurately define it.

The higher the form of life, the greater this element of mystery becomes and the greater becomes that realm of life through which our mind is unable to penetrate. Since Christianity is the highest form of life, it will not surprise us to find that in it we come in contact with the greatest of all mysteries.

In trying to speak briefly about the mysterious element in Christian life, I shall by no means endeavor to make the irrational rational, nor seek to explain the inexplicable. Permit me to concentrate our attention about the following points:

First, that there is a mysterious element in Christianity. Second, wherein does the mystery lie? And, third, how can this mysterious element be experienced?

*

Christianity has, from the very beginning, maintained that it possesses a life which is qualitatively different from all other forms of life.

This qualitative difference is brought out in various ways in the New Testament.

We read, for instance: "Wherefore if any man is in Christ, he is a new creature" (II. Corinthians 5:17). Here the apostle expresses the common and well known Christian truth that something qualitatively new has been created in every Christian. The same apostle even says that a new man has been created (Ephesians 4:24).

Christians have a common conviction that they are the possessors of a new kind of life, not found outside of Christianity; and in which no one can share unless he becomes a Christian.

We see in the New Testament that the impartation of this life, this new creation, is a fruit of the Messianic salvation. More closely defined, it is a fruit of that fundamental Messianic gift, the gift of the Spirit. It is the Messianic giving of the Spirit which mediates this new life.

Therefore, too, the apostle distinguishes sharply between the Spirit-born, the pneumatic man, and the non-Spirit-born, whom he calls the psychic or the natural man. That the apostle conceives of this difference as a qualitative one, a difference in kind, we see clearly from his words in I. Corinthians 2:14: "Now the natural man receiveth not the things of the Spirit of God: for they are foolishness unto him, and he can not know them, because they are spiritually judged."

Seen from this fundamentally apostolic view-point, it becomes clear to us why the New Testament writers used the strongest words which their language possessed to designate the difference between a Christian and a non-Christian. It is, they say, a difference as between life and death. "And you did He make alive, when ye were dead through your trespasses and sins" (Ephesians 2:1). Or: "We know that we have passed out of death into life, because we love the brethren" (I. John 3:14).

For this reason, too, salvation is called a raising up from the dead (Ephesians 2:6; 5:14).

In other contexts this qualitatively new thing is brought out by means of an even more graphic expression, namely, birth.

It is said of the Christians that they "are begotten of God" (I. John 3:9). And this "by the word of truth" (James 1:18), or "through the gospel" (I. Corinthians 4:15). This birth is referred to as a birth number two, in Greek: palingenesia (Titus 3:5; I. Peter 1:3, 23).

This birth is different from our first birth, our natural birth. The reason for thus differentiating between them is to emphasize the fact that no one becomes a Christian through the natural birth.

The reason that the first birth can not mediate that unique life which is known as the Christian life is that the first birth is "of the flesh." "That which is born of the flesh is flesh," while only "that which is born of the Spirit is spirit" (John 3:6).

*

Here we come in contact with the mysterious element in Christianity. The Christian church, from the days of the apostles and down to our day, has recognized the Spirit-born life as the real secret of its existence.

The Scriptural thoughts cited above also show that the mysterious element in Christianity is most intimately bound up with the supernatural element in Christian life. Because the Christian life is supernatural in its origin, it is also supernatural in kind.

The Christian knows that his life has been touched by

God in a supernatural way, that is, in a way that natural morality and religion is not able to affect him and, therefore, in such a way that no religion or system of morality can affect him.

Christians neither deny nor underestimate the value of other religious life. But they do maintain categorically and unequivocally that only the Christian religion imparts life in God, that is, that only through Christ can men be saved and enter into fellowship with God.

This is clearly stated in the New Testament in a number of passages. Jesus says: "No one cometh unto the Father but by me" (John 14:6). Because "neither doth any one know the Father save the Son, and he to whomsoever the Son willeth to reveal him" (Matthew 11:27). And the apostle bears witness: "And in none other is there salvation: for neither is there any other name under heaven, that is given among men, wherein we must be saved" (Acts 4:12).

This does not mean that it is in accordance with the Christian faith to say that other religions have no significance. On the contrary, in the last instance these, too, are from God and are intended as a preparation for the one saving religion. God has endowed man with a religio-ethical disposition, "that they should seek God, if haply they might feel after Him and find Him" (Acts 17:27).

However, none of the non-Christian religions lead to fellowship with God. All of them, the more advanced as well as the more primitive, represent natural man's attempt to think, feel, and demand God and the eternal realities. They are important insofar as they incline men toward that "fulness of time" when God, after a preparation covering thousands of years, could meet the religious aspirations of man and, through the suffering and death of His Son for man's sins, afford man access, not only to surmise, postulate, and worship God, but to live with God and to be received into fellowship with Him.

The mysterious element in Christianity is, therefore, this, that the Christian is certain that he possesses that life in God of which other religions have only a more or less vague idea, but to which none of them have attained. The Christian is happy in the assurance that his religion does not consist in religious self-exertion, stretching himself upward toward a holy and distant God on high. The secret of his religion is that God himself has come down to him, has laid hold on him and lifted him into a most intimate and blessed fellowship with Himself.

Here, therefore, we touch the vital mystery in Christianity, that which makes a man a Christian, which transforms his religiosity into Christianity.

*

But here, too, we come in contact with Christianity's worst stumblingblock, its hardest saying.

From the very beginning it has been so. Allow me at this point to adduce the account of the first man who felt this stumblingblock:

"Now there was a man of the Pharisees, named Nicodemus, a ruler of the Jews: the same came unto Him by night and said unto Him, Rabbi, we know that Thou art a teacher come from God, for no one can do these signs that Thou doest, except God be with him.

"Jesus answered and said unto him, Verily, verily, I say unto thee, except one be born anew, he can not see the kingdom of God.

"Nicodemus saith unto him, How can a man be born when he is old? Can he enter a second time into his mother's womb and be born?

"Jesus answered, Verily, verily I say unto thee, Except one be born of water and of the Spirit, he can not enter into the kingdom of God. That which is born of the flesh is flesh; and that which is born of the Spirit is spirit. Marvel not that I said unto thee, Ye must be born anew" (John 3:1-7).

This simple little account shows us clearly how the statement concerning the new birth and the new life threw the pious and noble Nicodemus completely out of equilibrium. We see this most clearly from the question he asked as to whether regeneration was to take place by his entering a second time into his mother's womb and being born again. This question was either foolish or impudent. In either event it shows that Nicodemus had lost his mental poise.

Let us try to put ourselves in his place and see how it must have affected Nicodemus.

He was a Jew. The average Jew awaited the Messiah and the establishment of the kingdom of God, at which time God would set free his oppressed people and show all the world that He is God and there is none beside Him. Israel was to become a world-ruling people; Jerusalem, the capital city of the world. The Gentiles were to be hewers of wood and drawers of water in this glorious and mighty kingdom. That the people of Israel were to be citizens of this kingdom was self-evident; of that every Israelite was firmly convinced. Publicans and brazen sinners, who boldly disobeyed the revealed will of God, were, of course, not to be admitted. They were to be given their portion with the Gentiles when the Messianic judgment was consummated.

And now Jesus says that no one, without exception, can enter the kingdom of God except he be born again!

The fact that one belongs to the house of Israel does not exempt him!

Nicodemus was not only an ordinary Jew. He was a Pharisee. That means that he belonged to that group in Israel which took its religion most seriously. It is true, as Jesus says, that the Pharisaic party of His day had fallen deeply both morally and religiously, and he reproved the Pharisees strongly for their hypocrisy; but Jesus has never said that all the Pharisees were hypocrites. From what we read in the New Testament about Nicodemus we can understand that he was no hypocrite, but, on the contrary, one of the noblest figures we meet in the religious life of that time.

Furthermore, Nicodemus was highly respected within the Pharisaic party. He was a member of the Sanhedrin, in truth a select company.

He is now told by Jesus that it does not help him that he is a Jew and a Pharisee and a member of the Sanhedrin of the chosen people. He can gain entrance into the kingdom of God only by being born anew.

That was what was so unintelligible and such a stumblingblock to Nicodemus.

Permit a little Biblical phantasy.

Suppose that Jesus had answered Nicodemus about as follows: "You have made a good beginning. You take your membership in the chosen people of God seriously, submitting to the holy law of God and living according to it in all things, the small as well as the great.

"Now you come to me and ask me if there is anything more that you must do in order to inherit eternal life. To this I would say: You pray three times each day. That is well. But it would be still better if you prayed six times each day.

"You give a tithe of all your earnings. That is well, because that is exactly what the law requires. But since you ask my advice, I would say: Give twice as much.

"You fast twice a week. That is well, for by so doing you do more than the law requires. My advice, however, would be that henceforth you fast four times a week. That will rightly prepare your heart for the great kingdom age which we can look for at any moment now."

Had Jesus answered Nicodemus thus, I can imagine that the latter would have gone home towards morning happy and contented, saying to himself: "This remarkable rabbi has a deep insight into everything. He is right also in this. I will begin even today to follow his good advice."

But when Jesus broke off his whole line of Jewish thinking about the law and the works of the law and told him that he would have to be born anew, then this good, pious man balked.

*

Since that night this has been repeated again and again down through the centuries.

No aspect of Christianity is more unintelligible and offensive to the natural man than the truth concerning the new birth. This soon becomes apparent to every one who speaks with his fellow men about these things.

In these days it is not easy to get people to talk about religion. It is not considered proper to speak about such things. It is proper and a sign of culture to speak about the weather or one's health, the latest betrothals or deaths, and the latest books or theatrical productions.

But suppose that we should succeed in engaging an ordinary, average, good, worldly person in religious conversation and suppose that we should speak to him in the following manner: "It seems to me that you ought to take your religion a little more seriously. You scarcely ever attend the house of worship. You must not continue in this way. Do come and hear the Word of God."

I think that a large number of these fine, worldly people would understand us and accept our well-meant little exhortation with good grace. They might even add: "Yes, you are right. I am not doing as well in this respect as I formerly did. And at times I have not felt just right about it. My conscience has often bothered me on Sunday mornings while I sat at home reading the newspapers. I will promise you that I will go to church."

On receiving such a friendly reply, we might perhaps take courage and say a little more: "You understand, of course, that it is not only a question of hearing the word; you must also be a doer of the word. You must begin to struggle more earnestly against your old, besetting sins. You take the name of God in vain every now and then. I have heard you do it a number of times this very day."

I can imagine that many of these good-natured, worldly people would answer: "Yes, you are right also in this. I must struggle more earnestly against my besetting sins. Have you really heard me take the name of God in vain? I thought I had gotten over that. However, now I am honestly going to quit."

After which we would perhaps get courage enough to say even a little more: "That is not all, either. You know that you are living only for yourself and family. You are no doubt a good provider and kind to the members of your household. But you know that it is not right to live such a selfish life as you are living. You must do a little for others also. You must take part in

Christian work, give to home and foreign missions, and support all good Christian enterprises in general."

Many of these good-natured, worldly people would admit also this: "You are no doubt in the right. I am too busy with myself and my own interests. But I shall try to be different in this respect from now on."

This is likely the answer that many a man would give. It is not at all unlikely, moreover, that one of them would take out his pocketbook and say: "Here is fifty dollars. I can not give more today. But I shall in the future contribute more to these causes than I have been doing in the past. Would you be kind enough to remind me of this from time to time? I forget so easily."

Most worldly people would understand a conversation such as this. A large number of them would also try to act accordingly, as far as they could.

But when we tell them that they must be born again, they balk exactly as Nicodemus did nineteen hundred years ago. They become irritated and even offended. They look upon this as something unreasonable. They say to themselves, and many of them say it also to others: "Can God require a person to do more than the best he can, namely, hear God's word, read, pray, struggle against one's besetting sins, and take part in and contribute toward Christian enterprises?"

Here we have the reason why these people approve of pastors who speak sternly about sin. After all, there are very few people in our country who like a worldly pastor, one who lets everything pass and who dishes out a milky mixture containing neither thought nor seriousness. People like those pastors who speak sternly and appealingly, best of all perhaps when the tears trickle down the cheeks of both the speaker and the listeners. Note well that this is the case only as long as the pastor speaks sternly and yet avoids mentioning conversion and the new birth, avoids making the Biblical distinction between regenerate and unregenerate men.

If he does that, people will, as a rule, have a large number of faults to find with the pastor. Of course, they never intimate that they are criticizing him because he speaks of conversion and regeneration. It would sound a little unreasonable to belittle him because he speaks the plain Word of God. Instead they bring up many other things about the pastor as a reason for not caring to hear him.

I can well understand that men who believe that it is possible to change and improve upon Christianity feel called upon to cut away these words about the new birth. It certainly is one of the greatest intellectual crosses in Christianity. They think that it will be easier to spread Christianity among the masses of the people if they remove this ancient and unreasonable idea.

However, that is not so easily done.

The essence of the matter is this: Christianity can not be changed. It is a fact. And it is well known that facts can not be altered, even though some people would like to do so and imagine that they are intellectually qualified to make the changes.

The great fact of Christianity is Jesus Christ as He is given us of God and proclaimed in the New Testament writings. And this fact can not, God be praised, be changed. A part of this fact is also the statement concerning the new birth. This truth will follow the Gospel of Jesus Christ to the end of time.

*

This is one of the points at which Christianity deviates

most sharply from all other religions and systems of morality. Take them all, the new as well as the old, theosophy, spiritism, anthroposophy, suphism—and what all they call these Oriental cults. And take the newest religious innovations which hail from those two countries which excel in inventions of all kinds: Germany and America. Take rationalism, liberal theology, Christian Science and Russelism.

No matter how they may differ, they have one thing in common: they believe in once-born religiosity only. They admit that man is in a sense sinful, but deny that he is wicked. And they all tell us that eventually man will become good. Do good and you will reach perfection.

Christianity occupies a unique position with respect to all these cults. It says: You are wicked. You can not do anything that is good before you yourself have become good. For it is the attitude of our heart which makes an act good or bad.

Jesus says expressly that He does not expect to gather figs from thorns. An evil tree can not bring forth good fruit. That is why He told Nicodemus that he must be born again and be given that new heart which is necessary in order to do good deeds and speak good words.

We can say, therefore, that this statement concerning the new birth is the greatest moral cross which has been put before the world, the highest moral ideal. It deals with the very foundation of moral life, the attitude of the heart. It is not satisfied with acts that are outwardly correct or words that sound well. It inquires concerning the attitude of the heart, the source of all our sayings and doings. If the attitude of the heart is not right, Christ calls an act evil, even though it may appear to be both pious and self-sacrificing.

But at the same time, this passage concerning the new birth is the most beautiful Gospel message which a sinner can hear. If we have come to realize that our heart is evil and if we have found that we ourselves can not change this wicked heart of ours, then it is indeed a beautiful message which is proclaimed to us when we are told that we are to receive a new heart, receive it as a gift from God.

Furthermore, we are to receive our new spiritual life in the same way in which we received the gift of natural life. It was given to us by others, without our moving a finger. Thus we are also to receive our new spiritual life by birth, by a new birth. God promises to put this new life into our hearts.

That was what Jesus wanted to tell Nicodemus that night long ago. And that is what He wants to tell all poor and helpless sinners today.

*

At this point there is an exceedingly great amount of misunderstanding.

It is, perhaps, no exaggeration to say that in this world of misunderstandings no one has been as terribly misunderstood as God. And God has not been misunderstood so badly on any point as that which deals with the question of becoming a Christian. Indeed, the misunderstanding here is greater than most people suspect.

If we should ask ordinary, average worldly people what it means to become a Christian, their answers would vary somewhat as to form, but the substance would be the same and would be about as follows:

"Well, this is what happens. A man becomes restless and unhappy and can no longer be glad and enjoy life, due either to sickness, sorrow, poverty, or old age. This inner unrest compels him to seek peace with God. And the God to whose will he must conform his life is a severe and exacting Lord. The least He requires is this:

"You must quit practically everything from which you derive any pleasure, such as dancing, drinking, card-playing, the theater, and the society of congenial and interesting people, if these people are worldly. And then you must begin to do things which you do not care to do at all. You must go to church and hear sermons which have a beginning but scarcely an ending. You must read the Bible, which is, of course, a good book, but exceedingly tiresome, because you have already heard everything that it contains. You must pray to God every day, yea, several times a day, if the Lord is to be satisfied. You must begin to associate with these believers or 'Bible readers,' who, as a rule, are good people but helplessly stupid, narrow, and tiresome. For they must, of course, always sing and read and pray when they get together. And you can never get a sensible word out of them about ordinary things."

That is, I believe, about the answer you would get.

I am prepared to hear some one raise the objection that I have exaggerated the matter somewhat.

But this is no exaggeration. Every worldly minded person is a proof of what I have said. They will not repent, even though most of them are convinced that they must change from the life they are now living.

Why will they not repent?

Simply because they look upon Christianity as an evil, a necessary evil to be sure, but, at all events, an evil, which should be avoided as long as possible. Therefore they postpone their conversion as long as they possibly dare.

They would rather "enjoy life," as they say, while they live. Then when they become ill or reach old age, have an accounting with God, receive the Sacrament of the Altar, die a nice death, have a beautiful funeral sermon preached by the pastor, and enter directly into eternal bliss.

Most people look upon such a life as the ideal, the best way of making the most of life's opportunities. Their lives prove it.

To them Christianity is an onerous burden, a yoke beneath which they must bend in order to satisfy the Lord. Here we are at the very core of the misunderstanding.

In days past believers were called hypocrites, without qualification and without exception. It was taken for granted that believers were inwardly exactly like other people, with no desire to read or speak about God or pray to Him. It was also assumed that the believers retained precisely the same desire as they formerly did toward a worldly and sinful life. The only difference, therefore, was this, that the believers pretended to be better than others by feigning a desire for God which they did not have and an aversion for sin which they likewise did not possess.

Nowadays there are not so many worldly people who say this as openly as they said it in days past. But that they still think it, is shown by their fear of becoming Christians. They look upon earnest, vital Christianity as a heavy yoke, as an unnatural life, in which one must stifle life's natural desire for happiness, and live a life in which neither head nor heart can enjoy the things they are supposed to enjoy.

I have read about a terrible instrument of torture

known as the Spanish coat. It resembled a coat and was put on the wretched victim in order to compel him to renounce his faith. The coat was made so that it could be screwed together tighter and tighter. If the victim refused to renounce his faith, his tormentors would keep on applying the screws until life was crushed out of the wretched man.

That was terrible, indeed. But if Christianity was what the ordinary man thinks it is and as I have just described it, it would be an even more terrible instrument of torture, a Spanish coat by means of which all natural human life would be pressed out of people. And think of never being able to get rid of it, but to be compelled to endure it for a life time!

How strange that people can think such thoughts about God! He who so loved the fallen race of men that He left glory and became a man! And as a man He suffered through thirty-three long years for our sake, until He had given His last drop of blood on the cross. That He should do anything so gruesome toward the poor children of men!

If only ignorant people had such ideas, the whole thing would be easier to understand. But that is the way many people think who otherwise exercise sound and practical judgment. That is what makes the thing so unintelligible. It shows that this way of thinking has originated in the nether regions and comes from him who is the sworn enemy of both God and man.

*

However, the religious life described above never has been true Christianity, although one runs across it now and then even yet. It is a common imitation of real Christianity. People do not care to pay the price of true

Christianity. It can not be had except through repentance and the new birth, which is exactly what people desire to avoid. But they do want to be considered Christians. So they try in their own strength to read the Bible, pray, and go to church. Likewise, they force themselves to renounce the things which they see believers renounce.

Naturally this becomes a hard, onerous life, full of compulsion and fear and without inner joy and willingness of spirit. If a child grows up in a home where such an imitation of Christianity as this blights not only the spiritual life of the parents but also the home atmosphere, it is easy to understand how such a child may come to cherish a deep aversion for and hatred of Christianity.

In case this book has fallen into the hands of such a person, permit me to say: You are entirely mistaken in believing that that is Christianity. I can, of course, account for your mistaken viewpoint: you have perhaps not had an opportunity to observe true Christianity at close range. Consequently, you have not had the opportunity of making comparisons. As a result you have taken what you have seen for what it was claimed to be, namely, true Christianity. But it was not.

It was, on the contrary, unregenerate man's attempt to serve God with the old, unwilling heart. Such a worship of God is as diametrically opposed to Christianity as it is possible to find. It is a worship of God which lacks that inner attitude of heart which is the vital mystery in Christianity and which gives the Christian's relationship to God its essential truthfulness and its joy.

You can become a Christian only by a divine miracle. Jesus calls this miracle the new birth. By that is meant the supernatural impartation of that life which is God's

life, that life which is holy. That life we did not receive
at our physical birth, for the reason that the human race
through the fall has lost vital connection with God.

This supramundane or heavenly life was brought to
our earth again by God through His Son. Now all who
hear the Gospel may share in it, if they will. But to do
so they must experience the second birth.

This miracle consists in this: God creates us new
within. He creates within us a new heart. We again
rejoice in God and in the will of God. The moral com-
mandments are no longer a demand upon conscience which
we would prefer not to heed or at best submit to unwillingly, but have become the law and delight of life, a law
which we with an inner desire and joy seek to fulfill.

It is this miracle which I should like to discuss.

I know, of course, that no man can understand a
miracle and can not, therefore, explain it. And that is
not what I have in mind. But I would like to speak
briefly about the experiences we have when God performs
the miracle of the new birth in our hearts.

Behold the sinner standing before God. He has seen
the condition of his own heart, and knows from experience that he does not love God and does not hate sin.
He has also tried hard to convert himself. That means
that he has tried to change his own heart; for conversion
is, of course, a change of heart. In this he has not been
successful.

With all the energy of his soul he has tried to make
himself love God. But, honest as he is, he must admit
that he is tired of reading the Bible, although he forces
himself to do it every day. He is also compelled to admit
that he has no desire to pray, although he prays every
day, because he knows that without prayer all is lost.

He is compelled to admit, furthermore, that he loves sin. In truth, he says to himself, I wonder if there is a single sin which I do not love if I could only commit it without incurring its harmful consequences.

He has now reached the point where he is at a loss to know what to do. Then in despair, but with unimpeachable honesty, he tells the whole dreadful truth to God: "Dear God, thou seest that I love sin and that I am unable to overcome this sinful love. And Thou seest that I do not love Thee. I tremble when Thou art near. And I am indifferent toward Thee when Thou art far away. I can not change this. I am eternally lost if Thou dost not help me."

Then the miracle takes place.

God lifts this sinful wretch up from the mire and washes him white in His own blood. Permit me to use the rich and picturesque figures of the Bible. He opens the book of heaven and strikes out all the sins which are written there, the one after the other. He casts them behind His back into the depths of the sea, to remember them no more. Then He opens the book of life and enters the sinner's name among those of all the other children of God.

Then He takes the trembling soul and lifts him into His lap, folds His eternal arms about him, and whispers into his aching, anxious soul: "You are My child now. Be not afraid. Once there was a reason for your fear and trembling, but not now. You are dead unto sin. And I live that I may help you in life, in death, and in judgment. My grace is sufficient for thee. You need nothing else. I am your Friend and Protector."

The bewildered sinner can not grasp or comprehend this at once. He sits in the lap of God and weeps bitter tears. Now and then he sees a few gleams of light, but most of the time all is dark to his inner eye. However, it is true of him as it was of Asaph: "My flesh and my heart faileth; but God is the strength of my heart and my portion forever" (Psalm 73:26). No matter what may come, he clings to God in earnest prayer and confession.

Then it comes to pass.

Light from above falls into the darkness of his soul. He sees everything in the full light of heaven. Jesus has died for his sins. He is a child of God. He does not need anything besides his Saviour. It is as though his heart would burst with joy! He gives thanks, he sings praises and songs of joy to the wonderful God who saves sinners.

Now no one needs to tell him to love God. His soul is full of grateful love to God. Spiritually speaking, he nestles himself close up to God, even as a little child throws its arms about its mother's neck upon her return from a long, long journey.

*

Here we are about as close to the heart of the mysterious element in Christianity as it is possible to get.

To be a Christian means to have the great privilege of living one's life close to the heart of God. God Himself has, through the new birth, lifted us up to this new plane of life. And we ask triumphantly: Is it difficult to love Him when we know Him so well?

Something new has now entered your heart. You love God. That is the new, the decisive thing. That was what was lacking before. Then you were afraid of God and tried to make yourself love Him. Or you were indifferent toward Him and tried to force yourself to respect Him enough to do as He commanded.

Now you are happy in God. You do not have to force yourself to seek Him in prayer or to read His Word. On the contrary, your most delightful hours are spent in so doing. You love the secret chamber. You almost steal away from people to be alone and undisturbed with God. You feel that you are in your proper element when you are with God. Like the fish in water.

It is the same mysterious element which we find in other spheres of life. At the home of a friend you meet a beautiful little child. You and the child become intimate, and you two prattle and play most gleefully. You and the little one agree that the child is to go home with you. To this the child readily consents. Now you two have a real good time. You give the child delicacies and candy, and you play together.

But after a little while the child grows very quiet. You offer it some more candy. All is well again. But soon the little one stops abruptly and cries out: "Where is my mother? I want to go to my mother!" It would not help now to have a whole house full of candy. The child wants to go to its mother, even though there may not be a single piece of candy at home.

Why? Because the child was born of its mother to be with its mother. That is the whole secret. So it is with every one who is born of God. He is born unto God to be with God. He feels happy when he is where God is, even though he can not always be speaking with Him. Just like the little child; the child can not be talking to its mother all the time, even though it is adept at prattling and thinking out loud.

It is the experience of God which is the real heart and secret of Christianity. As long as one merely thinks about God, postulates God, longs for and reaches out after God, one's relationship to God will, in the main, be a chaos of theoretical and practical problems. From the moment, however, that a man experiences God, all this is entirely changed. Paul has expressed it in these words: "Wherefore if any man is in Christ, he is a new creature: the old things are passed away; behold, they are become new!" (II Corinthians 5:17.)

We might say that this lies in the very nature of the case. We are created to experience God and to live our lives in the presence of God. And God is such that if we will but experience Him, everything else in our life will become properly orientated. For our hearts have been made right, which gives us the necessary prerequisite for taking the right attitude in all of life's relationships.

God is such that He takes captive and lays hold on our heart and thus binds us unto Himself. We become occupied with Him instead of with ourselves. When His love for us becomes something that we have not only read or heard or talked of, but something we have experienced, it fills our soul and gives it a new content. We also enter into a new relationship toward sin.

*

God Himself has no other means of overcoming our sin than to give us Christ. By accepting and experiencing Christ we receive the antidote which overcomes the poison of sin within us. If we have experienced Christ as our Saviour and have been given to see that we have in Him the gracious forgiveness of all sins, then we have that grateful love toward Him which overcomes our sin from within.

We begin to notice that it pains us to do anything against Him. Just as a child has no better safeguard against disobedience than its love of father and mother, so love of God becomes the believer's best safeguard against temptation.

With the new birth God puts into our heart a new moral power, which enables us to wage warfare in a new way against our old sins. The worldly man, too, struggles against sin; but in a worldly way. That is, he strives against sin because of the unpleasant and unprofitable consequences of sin. Sin itself he loves, but he must discipline himself into abstaining from it, because by sinning he brings injury upon himself.

With the new birth this too is changed. We now hate sin itself. The fact that our sin is against God is now the worst thing about it.

Understand me rightly. I do not mean that regenerate man is sinless. As long as we live here on earth "the flesh lusteth against the Spirit, and the Spirit against the flesh," as the apostle says (Galatians 5:17). The believer will, consequently, also after the new birth, experience a lack of desire for the Word and for prayer and an unwillingness to do the will of God. He will also have the painful experience of lusting after sin.

But he knows the apostle's comforting words to all earnest souls: "if any man sin, we have an Advocate with the Father, Jesus Christ the righteous: and he is the propitiation for our sins" (I John 2:1-2). And not only that, he knows, too, that the only way of overcoming sin is to experience anew the love of God in his heart. Therefore, he goes directly to his Saviour and tells Him the truth, that he does not love God, but sin. He asks Him out of sheer mercy alone to take him back to His heart and warm his lukewarm soul through and through with His wonderful love.

This is the real secret of sanctification, which does not come to pass by the will of the flesh, nor by the will of man, but by God alone. More definitely expressed, it is only the experience of God which can set the believer right again with respect to sin, when he through unfaithfulness or disobedience has fallen back into his old sinful ways.

The apostle of love exclaims: "Behold what manner of love the father hath bestowed upon us, that we should be called children of God" (I John 3:1).

Let us for a moment dwell upon that grace of God which saves us into childship with Him. He does not want us as slaves, who tremble at their master's voice and who carry out even the least of His commands unwillingly. Nay, He transforms His former enemies into friends. He delivers us from the spirit of bondage and gives us the spirit of adoption whereby we cry: "Abba, Father!" and by which we experience love's innermost desire: to ascertain and to carry out the will of the loved one.

What grace from God that He saves us in this manner! Christianity brings inward deliverance and joy to man. The Christian life is, therefore, the truest and best life that a man can live.

Let us consider somewhat more in detail this gracious aspect of God's salvation.

By His tender love He woos us away from our sin and our old life. Can you think of anything more beautiful! With the glow of love He melts the chains which bind us to sin. With His unfathomable love He beckons us to cast ourselves directly into His open arms. And with the same love He gives us courage to tell Him the truth and confess everything to Him.

From now on He can begin to reveal to us the full glory of the invisible world. Lovingly He beckons us to enter farther and farther into it. And the more we experience in this divine realm, the easier it becomes for us to renounce sin and the more scrupulous we become with regard to all evil. We experience a new and rich life, which enables us willingly and gladly to surrender the old life. "O the depth of the riches both of the wisdom and the knowledge of God!"

*

This vital element of mystery in Christianity has analogies in other realms of life. A little boy sits on the floor playing with his toys, as occupied as if there were nothing else in this world but his little boy-doll. If you take the doll away from him, he will cry and be very sorrowful. To him it seems as though you have taken his very life away from him.

But wait awhile, until he becomes twelve or fifteen years of age, for instance. Now give him his old plaything, and you will see him blush to the tip of his hair and throw it as far away as he can. What has happened? He has outgrown his toys, of course. He has reached a new plane of life, where he neither needs nor cares for them. Other things interest him now and occupy him even more thoroughly than his playthings formerly did.

The man who has been born again has also reached a new plane of life: the life of God, the holy life. Much of that which he formerly deemed indispensable, he has no use for any longer. He has a new purpose in life. His life has been filled with a new content. His interests lie on a different plane. For that reason, too, many things which formerly irritated him and even offended him, have now become his life and joy. Let me illustrate by an example close at hand.

This man's daily work now becomes new to him. Before this, it had been a burden, as a rule. It was especially difficult to practise fidelity toward it. He yielded usually to the temptation of getting out of his day's work as easily as possible. Often he caught himself stealing time and watching the clock. A remarkable change has occurred. In living his life as before God, his daily work, too, has taken on a different aspect. He feels intuitively that he is working for God even when he is doing the most menial task.

This exalts his labors and fills his working hours with something unspeakable. Often he can be so happy in the midst of his daily work that he experiences a joy fully as rich as that which he finds in the secret chamber or in the sanctuary.

In the next place, it makes him a more capable and a more industrious worker. The more he lives his life as before God, the less he feels tempted to steal time and to work only when watched. And the happier he is in his work, the better work he does.

Little thought is given to this phase of Christianity in our day. The New Testament, however, emphasizes strongly this new element which enters into a person's daily work when he becomes a Christian. Luther, with his clear, spiritual vision, uncovered again also this pearl of the Christian faith.

Few things, indeed, in a Christian's life are of greater importance than this: to have one's daily work exalted and put upon a higher plane.

In our day but few seem to succeed in this. Most people look upon their daily work as a burden. This burden becomes still more onerous when they imagine that it prevents them from "sacrificing themselves" for God and serving Him. They think that the only work they can do for God is the work they do outside of their secular calling, such as taking part in religious meetings, in societies, in singing, in testifying, in preaching, and in board and committee meetings of various kinds.

Such work is, of course, both good and necessary. There must always be some who stand ready to do these things in the kingdom of God. The misunderstanding arises, however, when people think that these are the most important and even the only work that can be done for God. On the contrary, of all the work we do for God first and foremost in importance must at all times be the doing of our daily tasks as before Him. In this way we are to "let our light shine before men; that they may see our good works and glorify our Father who is in heaven" (Matthew 5:16).

Not until then have we grasped the significance of real spiritual service, which, according to Paul, consists in "presenting our bodies a living sacrifice, holy and acceptable to God" (Romans 12:1).

That this service is of utmost importance in promoting the kingdom of God in our homes, in our communities, and in our whole country, I shall not discuss in detail at this point. Permit me, however, to point out how important it is to the believer himself to have his workaday life lifted up to this new plane.

Every normal person spends the greater part of his day at work. If his work is a burden to him, possibly even altogether distasteful to him, anyone can understand what an unhappy life his must be from day to day. We do not become victorious and happy Christians until we do our work as before God, until we experience the nearness of God in our daily tasks. Not until then does our whole life become a service, as God intended it to be.

*

Through the experience of God gained in the new birth, the difficult question of the Christian's relation to the world is also solved.

Is it sin to dance, to play cards, to attend the theater, or to be present at worldly functions? These questions often become the starting point of heated discussions. And it is difficult to arrive at any definite conclusion, because so much can be said both for and against them.

We will never get a clear and definite answer to these questions as long as the questions themselves are stated wrong. When the questions are put in the aforementioned way, they arise, as a rule, from an erroneous way of thinking and from a wrong attitude toward Christ.

An illustration. Two young people love each other and are living for each other. Suppose that some day the young man should ask his betrothed if it would be wrong for him to flirt a little with other young women. Only a little, he adds, hoping to placate both his betrothed and his own conscience. To this we would all say unhesitatingly: There is something wrong with that young man. The mere fact that he asks such a question is enough to show that his love for his betrothed is gone. For one who is in love does not ask himself how much attention he can give to other girls. He asks rather: How can I best serve her whom I love and make her happy?

Likewise, he who has had the love of God shed abroad in his heart and no longer has that slavish fear of God which desires to do His will as little as possible, but has become a happy child of God, does not ask: How far dare I venture out toward those things which are dangerous or forbidden without losing the favor of God? Nay, he turns the question right around: How can I best honor, please and serve my precious Saviour?

Can I honor and serve my Saviour by dancing and playing cards? That is the real question, in this connection, for every earnest disciple of Jesus.

He who can answer yes to this question before the face of the Lord, he will have to try to serve his Saviour at the card table and in the dance hall. He who must answer no to this question and say: rather than serving my Lord and being a blessing to my fellow men in such surroundings, I feel, on the contrary, that I would be injuring myself and the most precious part of my life by so doing, he must desist from dancing and card playing, etc., even though friends and acquaintances assure him that it is not in the least sinful or dangerous. He will refrain, even though he gains the reputation of being narrow-minded and pietistic. To him it is more important to serve his Saviour than to please men.

This is true Christian liberty: "All things are lawful for me; but not all things are expedient. All things are lawful for me; but I will not be brought under the power of any" (I Corinthians 6:12). "All things are lawful, but not all things edify" (I Corinthians 10:23). "For though I was free from all men, I brought myself under bondage to all, that I might gain the more." "And I do all things for the Gospel's sake, that I might be a joint partaker thereof." "I buffet my body and bring it into bondage: lest by any means, after that I have preached to others, I myself should be rejected." "Give none offence, neither to the Jews, nor to the Gentiles, nor to the church of God" (I Corinthians 9:19, 23, 27; 10:32).

Have *you* life in God?

You may answer perhaps: "I was baptized as a child. I was instructed in the Christian faith. I pray and I read the word of God. I go to church and do church work as well as I can in my humble way."

All of which is good and well. But that is not what I am asking you. I am asking you if you have life in God, that is, if it is love which brings you to God, if you are living the free, joyous, and blessed life of a child of God? Or is it the onerous, unwilling life of the unregenerate heart that you are living with God?

Examine yourself. Be earnest. Your eternal destiny hinges upon the answer you give to this question.

Remember the plain words of Jesus: "Except one be born anew, he can not see the kingdom of God." "That which is born of the flesh is flesh."

Have you experienced what the apostle speaks of when he says: "Wherefore, if any man is in Christ, he is a new creature: the old things are passed away; behold, they are become new?"

Does your moral and religious life consist of what Scripture calls "dead works," that is, works which are good and proper, outwardly considered, but which do not spring naturally and vitally from a saved and grateful heart?

At this point many deceive themselves.

Today this form of self-deception lies closer at hand than has been the case for the last two generations. True, there has been awakened again a wide-spread interest in things religious after the religiously lean years of materialism. But there are too many who are satisfied with religiosity, being unwilling to press on through the narrow gate to real Christianity. They are content with seeking after God instead of persevering until they find and experience Him.

The temptation to do this is very great for many, because up to this time they have lived very far away even from religiosity. They think that because there has been somewhat of a change in their inner as well as in their outward life, therefore they have become Christians. The religious longings which they now experience and the religious activity to which they now feel impelled, such as prayer, reading, meditation, and Christian work, seem to them to constitute such a great change of heart that they think they have experienced Christian conversion.

For many it is very easy to make this mistake, because they are ignorant of what true Christianity is. This ignorance is quite general and very profound, especially among the higher classes of society. In very recent times this ignorance seems to have spread rapidly also among large numbers of the laboring classes.

I ask, therefore, again: Have you experienced the miracle of the new life? Have you been lifted by God Himself into a new relationship with Him? Or does your religion consist in worshipping and serving God with your old, obdurate and unwilling heart? Is your ethical life a requirement forced upon you by your conscience, a demand which you would prefer to ignore and to which you submit unwillingly at best; or has it by the divine miracle of regeneration become your life and your delight?

*

Perhaps some one of my readers is saying to himself: "I have not experienced this new creation. My religious life is a heavy, burdensome duty, which I often neglect and which I must force myself to perform. Often I do it in an absent-minded and spiritless manner.   Dead works!   That is without doubt the right name for my Christianity.

How can I get life in God?

What must be done on my part in order that God may perform this miracle within me?"

My friend, it is not difficult to tell you what you must do.   You have nothing to do but to turn to your Saviour and confess to Him that you love sin and not God, and ask Him to perform the miracle in your heart.

The moment you truly go to God in this way, He will perform the miracle of regeneration within you.

I am prepared to hear somebody say: "I have already done this some time ago.   But I did not experience what you have described above as the effects of divine regeneration.   I have not felt the nearness of God of which you speak.   Not the joy and bliss.   Nor the peace and inward calm.   Nor the dislike for sin.   Nor the desire to do God's will.   So far I have experienced practically nothing but restlessness and fear, now and then exceedingly great distress.   Between times I have had a few brief periods of calm.

What is the matter with me?

What shall I do further in order to experience what you have described?"

In reply to this, permit me to say, first, that every birth is a painful process.   Spiritual birth is no exception to the rule.   The spiritual pains you are experiencing, in the form of restlessness, doubt, fear, and anxiety, are birthpains.

The Holy Spirit of God is at work creating something new within you.   But the new life can not be born within you except the old die at the same time.   It is God who killeth and who maketh alive (Deuteronomy 32:39). Paul says in the account of his conversion that he died (Romans 7:9-10). He has reference to the painful process by means of which God through His holy law convicted him of sin, "that sin might become exceedingly sinful" to him (v. 13). Or, as he expresses it in another place, "that every mouth may be stopped and the sinner be brought under the judgment of God" (Romans 3:19).

What you are now experiencing in your spiritual distress and restlessness is this life's first beginning: death. Jesus Himself pointed out the organic connection between death and life in the familiar words about the grain of wheat which must fall into the ground and die before life can come forth from it (John 12:24).

You must first see the sin in your heart and life, which sin must die. Just to see this is a painful and fearful experience, enough to fill a soul with hopelessness and despair, because men do not realize how sinful they really are. This, too, Paul has described in a classical way: "I was alive apart from the law once: but when the commandment came, sin revived." "Sin, finding occasion, wrought in me through the commandment all manner of coveting" (Romans 7:9, 8).

This experience becomes still more painful when one not only sees the wickedness of one's life, but also discovers, when trying to battle against it, that one is not able to overcome one's sins, either in word or in deed, and still less in thought and fantasy. This, too, Paul has described: "I am carnal, sold under sin." "I know that in me, that is, in my flesh, dwelleth no good thing." "Wretched man that I am! who shall deliver me out of the body of this death?" (Romans 7:14, 18, 24).

If you have begun to have these inner experiences, do

not permit yourself to become frightened or confused. It is the Lord's work in your soul. It is painful, to be sure. All such curative experiences are distasteful to our pampered natures, but they are necessary. Give thanks to our merciful God, who in this way has begun to put to death your old life.

The disturbing experiences with yourself and with your sin through which you are passing, should not frighten you away from God. On the contrary, what God has shown you of your sin should rather drive you to your crucified Saviour, make you hunger for the grace of God and seek salvation, and become one of those whom the Lord calls blessed: "Blessed are they that mourn: for they shall be comforted. Blessed are they that hunger and thirst after righteousness: for they shall be filled. Blessed are the poor in spirit: for theirs is the kingdom of heaven" (Matthew 5:3-6).

After the Lord has put to death, He also makes alive.

Be calm, therefore. Let the Lord Himself take full charge of this work. He Himself will perfect the good work which He has begun in your soul. When He sees fit, the veil will be drawn aside, and you will rejoice in salvation with unspeakable joy. You will experience God's blessed presence, peace, and rest. You will be given an inward dislike of sin and a holy desire to do His will.

Meanwhile, wait humbly and patiently for the Lord. Plead your distress before Him each day. Read His Word and cling to His promises.

Remember this: You experienced the new birth the moment you turned to your Saviour and honestly confessed your sins. What you have felt so far has been principally its mortifying and painful aspects. But that, too, is a part of the vital mystery of Christianity.

BOOK FIVE

The Logic of Repentance

REPENTANCE, according to the New Testament, is the condition whereby man becomes a partaker in God's great gift to the human race: the kingdom of God.

Already in the time of John the Baptist this was made clear: "Repent ye, for the kingdom of heaven is at hand!" (Matthew 3:2). Jesus reiterated it: "From that time began Jesus to preach, and to say, Repent ye; for the kingdom of heaven is at hand" (Matthew 4:17).

When, on the Day of Pentecost, Peter, filled with the Holy Spirit had preached his first mission sermon, and the people had been convicted of sin and had begun to ask what they should do, he answered: "Repent ye, and be baptized every one of you in the name of Jesus Christ unto the remission of your sins" (Acts 2:37-38).

All of the apostles preached in the same way. See Acts 8:22; 11:21; 17:30; 26:18, 20; II Corinthians 3:16; 12:21; James 5:20; II Peter 3:9; Hebrews 6:1; Revelations 2:5, 21, 22; 3:19.

This was exactly what the Lord Himself had commanded them to do: "Thus it is written, that the Christ should suffer, and rise again from the dead the third day; and that repentance and remission of sins should be preached in His name unto all the nations" (Luke 24:46-47). He had also said that repentance was absolutely necessary in order to enter into the kingdom of God: "Except ye turn, and become as little children, ye shall in no wise enter into the kingdom of heaven" (Matthew 18:3).

*

I do not know, my dear reader, what your relation to God is. But I believe that I make no mistake when I take it for granted that you long for fellowship with God. Perhaps more, perhaps less, according to the varying times and circumstances in your life. You feel drawn toward God. You hope some day to succeed in finding peace with God. Above all else, you hope to turn to God in your old age, when you are to depart this earthly life, that you may go home to God, to the kingdom of glory, to eternal rest and peace after the ceaseless turmoil and strife of this life, with all its difficulties and hardships.

Nor do I think that I take too much for granted when I assume that you have had many wonderful experiences with God, precious moments when God drew very near to you. The things of this world faded in significance, while the world of eternal things pervaded your soul with remarkable reality and with an almost irresistible attraction. You felt insignificant and very small when you stood in the presence of our great and holy God, and you felt that you were extremely unclean and sinful. Small and great sins came to mind and crowded before your inner eye. There was something strangely solemn about it all. You had nothing to offer in your own defense, no way of concealing yourself. It was like standing unarmed and unshielded in a hailstorm of bullets.

Instinctively you folded your hands. Perhaps you bent the knee also. And you began to cry to God. Everything was strange, and you scarcely recognized yourself. The following day, as you thought of it, you felt somewhat uncertain of yourself. You were glad that no one knew what had happened. Now and then you were tempted to look upon it as a case of overstrained nerves. But deep down in your heart you were convinced that you had never been yourself at any time as much as in that wonderful and holy hour in the presence of God.

You have, perhaps, not had many such experiences. But your longings have been awakened, and you love to occupy yourself at frequent intervals with religious thoughts and to read religious literature. Little by little, too, you have come to the point where you desire to be perfectly clear in the matter of your relationship to God.

Listen: Christ is your divine Friend. He is not what you have often been tempted to think that He is: reticent, cold, and unmerciful. He is your Friend and is therefore interested in you. He is interested in having things made clear to your own mind concerning your relationship to God, in order that you might become a free and happy Christian.

*

He tells you clearly and plainly: "Except ye turn, and become as little children, ye shall in no wise enter into the kingdom of heaven."

I am certain that I do not presume too much concerning you when I take it for granted that you acknowledge the absolute authority of Jesus. You fully recognize Him as the only one who is perfectly qualified to deal with these questions. At least, I do.

Now, He says that repentance is the only way into the kingdom of God, into vital fellowship with God.

I can readily imagine that some do not recognize Jesus

in these words. Otherwise so gentle, kind, and full of understanding when dealing with sinners, here He seems so hard and stern: If a person be not repentant, he can have no part in the kingdom of God.

But we should remember that love is both gentle and stern. According to the Gospels, Jesus was not merely a gentle optimist, as many would make Him in our day. He was also a stern realist, who was faithful to the truth in love. His love was so great that He spoke the truth to all who would listen to it.

It was love, too, which prompted Him to speak the hard word about repentance. He saw how people were deceiving themselves, not least the religious people. Because they were religious, they thought that they were on the right path. But Jesus saw that, in spite of their morality and religiosity, they were on the broad way to perdition. He sees, too, how this self-deception is repeated in every age.

Accordingly, He steps into the midst of seething humanity and cries out with all the power of His love: That way will end in perdition. If you wish to go to heaven, turn about. There is only one way to heaven, the narrow way, which begins at the straight gate of repentance.

My reader, are you repentant?

This is an insistent question, it is true. But truth is insistent. And upon this question depends your eternal destiny.

If you are not repentant, you are unsaved, no matter how much you hope and wait and long and think and worry, even read and pray. This is the simple meaning of Jesus' quiet but earnest warning: "Except ye repent, and become as children, ye shall in no wise enter into the kingdom of heaven."

Are you repentant?

Perhaps you do not like the question.

There are many who can not become fully reconciled to this word about repentance. They think that it is too easy, too schematic, methodistic, and pietistic. They think it deals too roughly and ruthlessly with high and holy things.

Besides, they do not really like the people who say that they are converted. In the first place, they do not like to hear these people put themselves in a class by themselves and speak about others as being unconverted. They think that these people are a little too sure of themselves and conceited when they speak of themselves as people that are converted, that are children of God, that are regenerate believers. If they would only say that they would like to be children of God, and that they would like to be more and more believing, it would sound a little more modest, a little more humble. They are too great in their own eyes, too certain of themselves.

Have you had such thoughts about believing Christians? And have you talked like that about them?

Then may I ask you one thing: Have you not now and then had a feeling that you were doing them an injustice?

I recall that before my conversion I, too, thought and spoke in that way about believers. But I also remember that deep down in my heart I often had a suppressed feeling that I was unjust toward them. I understood that there was something about believers which I did not possess, although I, too, wanted to be looked upon as a religious man and even as a Christian.

Gradually it dawned upon me more and more that the difference between their religiosity and mine was this one thing: repentance. They had experienced repentance.

I had not. Why should it be wrong of them to say that they were converted?

If you were to ask me: "Are you married?" I would answer: "Yes, I am." If you were to ask me: "Are you converted?" I would answer: "Yes, I am." But, of course, in this case I would feel like adding: "By the wonderful grace of God."

If I have experienced repentance I must say so, and not say that I hope or desire to experience it. That would not be the truth.

Meanwhile, I can well imagine that you have met some folks who say that they have been converted, and yet they really are conceited and haughty. But they are not repentant, no matter how much they say they are. For Jesus says in the passage I have quoted above that they who turn to God become as little children, that is, become humble, not great, in their own eyes.

There is not a little of this non-genuine article, this imitation of true Christianity. Jesus Himself foresaw it, and prophesied that it would come. But, in the name of truth, you must not blame Christianity for that. If you meet people who have so little Christianity that they have become proud and conceited, you must try to help them, because they are deceiving themselves. You ought to go to them and say: " Your conversion will not bring you to heaven, because it has made you proud instead of humble."

*

I have thought a great deal about repentance, both before and since I was converted. There are perhaps few things which I have given as much thought.

I have said to myself: If Jesus had not made repentance the condition whereby we must be saved, would not perhaps more people have reached heaven? In fact, now and then I have asked myself if almost all of them would not have consented to be saved.

I have observed how religious everybody is, after all. Most people want to have at least some dealings with God, especially during adversity, illness, or old age. Even though they do not care to be particularly intimate with the Lord, yet they do not want to be at odds with Him. Therefore we notice that they go to church occasionally and even to the Lord's Supper. They contribute to missions and to other good causes. In a way they struggle against their sins, even though the opposition they put forth is not very great nor leads to very outstanding and decisive battles.

But I observe also that as soon as you mention a word from the Bible about repentance to these people, most of them balk. They can follow you no farther. Insistence upon repentance seems unreasonable to most of them; at least, it is an insurmountable something which they seek to evade in one way or another. Like those in the parable, who were bidden to the feast, they reply more or less courteously: Have me excused!—And proceed, more or less religiously, on their way to eternal perdition.

Now, I am certain that Jesus did the right thing when He made repentance the condition upon which admission into the kingdom of heaven is possible. He did not do it in order to make it difficult for men to be saved. He did it because it was absolutely necessary. Not even an almighty and all-loving God can save sinful men if they will not repent.

To me the question resolves itself into this: Why is repentance necessary before God can take us into His kingdom?

In order to arrive at an answer to this question, we must take as our starting-point the query: What is repentance? Repentance is a well-known and yet somewhat hazy expression. In the New Testament the word "metanoia" is used, which means about-mindedness or change of mind.

This little bit of information throws light at once upon the question we have raised. It tells us that there is something wrong with our mind, which, unless it is changed, makes it impossible for God to get us into His kingdom.

The question is now changed for the third time and reads as follows: What is there about our mind which makes it impossible for God to receive us into His kingdom without first changing it?

This question is very easy to answer as long as we think only of the openly ungodly. If a man has such a mind that he kills his neighbor, either out of desire for revenge or for gain, we all realize that he must have a change of mind. We simply can not live together with such people, and for that reason we put them in prison.

Or if a man has a mind to destroy women and children both physically and spiritually, we all realize at once that such perpetrators of immorality must have their minds changed. If not, because of the danger to society, they must be interned until it can be established that a real change of mind has taken place.

The question becomes more difficult when we turn to a consideration of those people, who in our country are, of course, in the majority—who are good, decent, honorable, useful, able, conscientious, generous, yea, even religious.

Is there anything wrong with them? Must they, too, have a change of mind?

I know full well that there are many who think that such people do not need to be converted. They think that such people need only to become more religious and more moral, that is, that it is only necessary for them to develop further along the same line. To speak to these people about repentance is looked upon as spiritual rudeness, as methodistic manhandling of souls, as pietistic narrow-mindedness and superficiality, which spring from fanaticism and which drive others into fanaticism.

I know, too, that even some pastors have this view with regard to repentance. For that reason they never draw the Biblical distinction, in their preaching, between the converted and the unconverted, between the children of God and the children of the world. In their preaching they proceed upon the theory that all their listeners are Christians, and treat them as such. To be sure, they recognize a difference between them, but only a difference of degree: some are zealous Christians, others less zealous.

I shall not take up this matter for discussion at this point. I assume that we all submit to Jesus Christ as the sole and final authority in things pertaining to salvation. His decision in the matter is as follows, and in clear, plain words: "that which is born of the flesh is flesh" (John 3:6). "Except ye turn, and become as little children, ye shall in no wise enter into the kingdom of heaven."

But, some say, these words of Jesus apply only to ungodly people. They can not be applied unconditionally to people who are baptized and confirmed and who live a good moral and religious life.

To this I must reply as follows:

First, Jesus and the apostles directed their exhortation about repentance not only to the ungodly, but also to the moral and religious people of their day. The words cited were spoken first to Nicodemus, one of the finest characters we come in touch with in the New Testament. Both Jesus and John the Baptist directed their admonition about repentance to their religious contemporaries. They could scarcely reach any of the others.

In the second place, it is true that there are people who, ever since the time of their baptism as infants, have been at home in the Father's household. They have remained in the grace of their baptism throughout their childhood years and up through the period of youth, until they entered into that conscious and direct relationship with God which adults have. However, they, too, have experienced conversion at one point or another during the transition from childhood to maturity. [1]

But a large majority of the people who have been baptized in infancy leave the Father's household, as the prodigal son did, and go into the far country. As soon as they reach the age when they determine their own inner life, they forsake the God of their childhood and their childhood faith. They do not care to live in fellowship with God, do not care to make an honest accounting of their sins each day before God. Consequently, they flee Him.

Let us notice that the Bible speaks of such people as having fallen from grace. They live a worldly and unrepentant life, away from God. They are children of the world, and not children of God, even though they have been baptized. The life that was given them in baptism they themselves have stifled and put to death. They are "dead in trespasses and sins," as Scripture expresses it. Jesus says about the prodigal son when he

---

[1]Those who desire further information concerning the conversion of the God-fearing child, I would refer to my book, "Infant Baptism and Adult Conversion," p. 68 ff.

returned: "This thy brother was dead, and is alive again" (Luke 15:32).

*

We come back to our question: Why must people who have been *such* decent, useful, good, religious people repent?

I am happy to know that the question is not as difficult to answer as might appear at first glance. Neither great ability nor a great deal of knowledge is required. The only thing that is necessary is that we honestly examine our own minds. That will give us as clear an answer as anyone could ask for.

We must look at the mind. Jesus has shown us that it is our attitude that counts both in morality and in religion. It was at this point that Jesus shed new and revolutionary light upon the moral history of mankind.

Jesus says that what makes an act good or bad, sinful or not sinful, is not the doing of it, nor its successful or unsuccessful outcome, but its motive, the impulse from which it springs.

Consequently, when Jesus passes judgment upon our religious relationships, He does not look only upon the religious acts which we perform: whether we go to church and to the communion table; whether we read, pray, do church work, strive against sin, etc. On the contrary, He looks first and foremost upon the heart from which these religious acts have issued. If our heart is right, He is exceedingly patient and longsuffering, even though our deeds are not as well done as they might be. But if our heart is wrong, none of our religious or moral acts have any value in His sight.

If you desire a few clear gleams of light into this view of Jesus with regard to religion and morality, read, for instance, Matthew 5:21-26; 6:1-6; 6:16-18. These passages show that Jesus does not accept as a sop a few correct religious ceremonies or mere outwardly moral conduct. He cuts straight through outward things and goes to the very secret motives of the heart.

The first part of the gracious work of salvation which Christ accomplishes in sinful man is this: to show him what his mind is like in a way that can not be denied, and to help him to understand that his mind, his attitude, must be changed, and that from the bottom up.

*

Let us now consider this briefly.

My reader, do you pray to God each day?

In reply many of my readers will no doubt say: "Yes, God be praised, I pray to God every day, some times many times a day! Otherwise I do not see how I could live my daily life."

But, no doubt, some will answer: "No, I do not pray quite every day. Is that really necessary? Does the Bible say anything about praying every day? Does God expect that? Now when there is so much to do and so little help to be gotten? That old and sick people pray a great deal, even every day, is natural, because they do not neglect anything by so doing. But we who are well, do we not please God more and perform a greater service by working diligently and conscientiously rather than by being on our knees a great deal in prayer? Are not busy hands more pleasing to God than folded hands?"

I do not know whether or not you have any further reasons for not praying every day. Nearly twenty-five years have passed since I busied myself with such reasons, and it is very possible that I have forgotten some of them.

My friend, study your own attitude calmly and quietly

and you will see at once what must be changed. You will see why repentance is necessary.

Your very attitude must be changed. You do not *will* to pray to God every day; that is the whole thing. Why not? Well, simply because you do not love God.

Without having the only thing which God desires to find in you, namely, love, you are striving to do what you know God ordinarily requires of Christians. And, like a lazy and unwilling schoolboy, you are trying to get a passing mark and yet do as little as possible. Furthermore, your unwillingness rises to new heights every time you realize that more morality and religion are required of you than you at present are able to produce.

And have you not in some quiet hour had a feeling that what you lacked as far as religion was concerned was the very essence of man's relationship to God: the willing and grateful surrender of the heart to God.

This is what Jesus sees. And for that reason He says to you as well as to other sinful men: "You must repent. You must have a new heart. I must create within you what you lack more than anything else: love to God.

*

Now a word to you who pray each day.

He who sees in secret rejoices that each day you enter into your chamber and shut the door. But here, too, it is your attitude which is the important thing. What does He see in you?

Does He see a heart which longs to be alone with its beloved? A heart which can not begin the day with its tasks, its struggles and temptations, without first having a quiet hour with the Almighty Friend?

Or does He see a heart which is distracted by many thoughts and has very little time for prayer? You bend the knee, and you fold your hands. You begin to speak with God. But you are soon through, because you have prayed that prayer so many times before. Meanwhile, your thoughts are occupied almost constantly with other things. However, you come to an end and say, Amen.

You have prayed! You feel easier. But your invisible Friend wonders, no doubt, what you wanted of Him, what you wanted Him to do for you. But you do not seem to realize that; you have already risen and are through praying.

Do you read the Bible daily?

In doing this, too, it is your attitude that God looks upon.

What did He see the last time you read the Bible? A heart which could not endure the thought of taking another step on the narrow and dangerous way of life without first being filled with the blessed, life-giving, regenerating word of God? Or a heart which distractedly and absent-mindedly turned to the same page in the Bible which you read last, read it again, perhaps finished the chapter, and then closed the Book and put it aside?

If somebody had asked you at the door of your room what the chapter was about, would it have been hard for you to answer?

When the good Lord sees this attitude, He says: This must be changed. All the forms are correct enough. Nothing is lacking in this respect, but the very heart of religion is absent. Now and then you have no doubt also felt, my religious friend, as you listlessly and unwillingly force yourself to pray, that you do not love God. Your heart is not in it, no matter how regularly you do it from day to day. You use words, but they are repetitious and perfunctory.

The Lord looks upon our *attitude,* our *mind.*

What does He see in you? He sees an ocean of sin and iniquity, bottomless and boundless. Think for a moment how you would feel if you were transparent and people round about you could see at all times what sinful desires, fantasies, and thoughts were going through your mind. You would, no doubt, fall into despair, or hide yourself like a hermit in order that no one might see you.

But God knows your attitude by night as well as by day. And it is for this reason that He tells you with all the power of His love: You must turn, your attitude must be changed.

Permit me to mention one thing more which shows the inner necessity of repentance.

How have you reacted to the authoritative message of the Bible about repentance each time it reached your conscience? In general, unconverted people react in one of two ways.

The one way out is to try to wriggle away from this truth. Men try to make themselves believe that things can not be as the Bible says they are. Is no one really saved except those who repent? Then there will be only a very few. Will God actually condemn all the rest? That is impossible, of course. Then He can not be Love. Neither can He be righteous if He condemns all these good honorable people merely because they have not been converted!

In our day we are accustomed to decide things easily and expeditiously by a majority vote. Standing before the Lord with an overwhelming vote on their side, these people feel fairly safe and say: He can not condemn so many of us!

Furthermore, there are many pastors who think that

conversion is unnecessary. Consequently, these folk take refuge beneath the pulpits of these preachers. There they will not be disturbed. If, in spite of everything, they do happen to hear a man who preaches the Biblical truth concerning repentance, they shield themselves fairly easily by saying to themselves and to others: These hell-fire preachers are a great curse to the church in our day. They scare people away from the Church and from Christianity. They should really not be allowed in the churches, but stay with the religious fanatics where they belong.

Thus they silence the voice of their own consciences, and persuade themselves to believe a lie.

The other way out, which unconverted people make use of when the Biblical message about repentance strikes them, is much more frequently used. Those who take this way do not try to explain away the truth of the Bible. They admit that repentance is necessary and that they themselves are not converted and, therefore, not saved. They acknowledge the truth, and say to themselves: I must be converted, and I will repent. There is really nothing that I am more in earnest about than that. But just now it is too inconvenient, too hard. I will, therefore, wait a while. Not long, only a little while, because then it will be so much easier.

My friend, have you had such thoughts? Many times, no doubt.

Have you not at times felt the insincerity of it? This is a case of inward guile which is very grave. And for that reason it is very dangerous.

You admit the truth of the Biblical admonition concerning repentance. But you will not repent. And in order to satisfy your conscience in the easiest possible way, you try to make yourself and God believe that you will repent, but not just now. This form of deception, practised by those who postpone their conversion, is very dangerous.

Jesus said on one occasion: Every one that is of the truth heareth My voice (John 18:37). This means that every one who is called by Jesus and does not heed His call, that is, does not repent, is not of the truth. He is practising deception, both toward himself and toward God. If it were true that he desired to be converted, he would not postpone it one single moment. This lies in the very nature of conversion.

The Lord sees this mind in you. And for that reason He says that your mind must be changed. It must be changed immediately. A man can not practise such inner deception very long before he will be hopelessly lost.

This is according to the very nature and the very laws of spiritual life.

He who has a clear, strong conviction and does not follow it out becomes first a weak character; thereupon, he loses his character completely. That is, he gradually loses the power of following out his convictions. A man thus devoid of character is, as a rule, a man of many and great plans, strong desires, pleasant dreams, and beautiful words. But every time he tries to realize some of them, some little thing always happens to him; something invariably intervenes, usually something very insignificant. But it is always enough to prevent him from following out his convictions.

What then? He lays new plans, develops new longings, dreams new dreams, and speaks more new words. But again he has some little mishap; some little thing goes wrong just as he is about to realize his new plans.

The life of the soul can not endure this. After a

person thus misuses and does violence to the soul's finest capacity, he loses all ability to have a conviction. By convictions we mean thoughts related so intimately to the life of our conscience that they drive the will in a definite way to translate these thoughts into action.

When a person loses the ability to have a conviction, all that remains to him is his dreams, longings, and thoughts, perhaps good thoughts too. But there is this about them, that they can no longer drive the will to make a definite decision. Like Peer Gynt, they always avoid this.

Then that soul is lost, hopelessly lost, even though the man leads an outward life which is not at all out of the ordinary. On the contrary, such people as a rule lead conventional lives and resemble the average man very closely.

Such a soul is hopelessly lost because not even God can save him. He has no other way of saving men than by convincing them. Jesus, too, said that it is the work of the Spirit to "convict of sin, of righteousness, and of judgment" (John 16:8). And when a person has reached a point where God has no way of convicting him and causing him to heed His call unto conversion, then that person is eternally lost.

And we have it from Jesus's own lips that when a person gets to that point, He gives him up. I am thinking now of His words in the parable of the barren fig tree (Luke 13:6-9). It is touching to hear Him intercede for the barren tree. When He prays that it be spared, it is because He can still point to some means whereby it may be saved. But He adds with solemn earnestness: if it does not bear fruit then, cut it down.

That is, a person is not given up until the Saviour has

tried all the means at the disposal of His power and love. As long as all these means have not been tried, that person lives, because Jesus intercedes for him. He prays life into him.

But when everything has been tried and nothing has brought repentance, then that person is lost. Listen to this, modern man, with all your doubts and misgivings. It is Jesus who says so, whom you, too, acknowledge as the sole authority in eternal things. He says so clearly and unmistakably. Read His words in Matthew 25:41, 46; 12:31-32; 5:29-30; Luke 12:5.

And cease employing that worn-out, meaningless argument that God would not be love if He suffered any one to be lost. I fear it will be a long time until we reach the stage when we will be in position to reproach Jesus for lack of love. You and I lack both truth and love. Jesus has both. He loved sinners so greatly that He died for us. And He loves us so much even now that He tells us the plain truth, even though it hurts.

He tells us truthfully that a person will be lost if he does not repent, that is, experience a change of heart and follow out the sacred convictions which he has received through the call of divine grace.

Observe: it is not because of lack of love that God suffers a person to be lost. It is because Almighty God Himself is impotent to help that soul which has destroyed itself and can no longer be saved. If you would like to learn a little of the love which Jesus has even for such people as have brought themselves into this spiritual state, read Luke 19:41-44. There we read that Jesus wept over the city which He knew had already hardened its heart and had nothing to look forward to but the judgment of God.

My friend, you who sit here today, weak, vaccilating, slothful and unable to come to a decision, consider for a moment the necessary, unavoidable consequences of a life in sin, and it will be easier for you to see the sacred logic of repentance.

*

I have not been engaged as an attorney for our Lord. He does not need us to defend Him. But I can not deny that I occasionally feel a desire to say a word about the reasonableness of Christianity.

Many in our day think that reason and Christianity are as incompatible as fire and water. Many even of those who are convinced that Christianity is necessary to salvation, think that it has very little to do with reason. I feel a desire, therefore, to point out the inner rationality and logic of Christianity. In this illogical and meaningless world of ours, I see at least one thing that is rational. And that is Christianity.

Permit me to say a word about this also while speaking on conversion.

When God makes repentance the necessary condition whereby we can be received into His kingdom, He does just what we would do under similar circumstances.

Some of my male readers are, no doubt, married or engaged to be married. Do you remember your courtship days? Perhaps it is a long time ago for some of you. But you will never forget the blissful moment in your life when you stammeringly told her that your heart was filled with love for her.

Suppose now that she had answered you about as follows: "Yes, I shall try. I shall do the best I can. I will live with you and work with you, make our home cozy, and save all I can for ourselves and our children.

But—you must from the outset remember that I love somebody else. And you must allow me to continue to love him. I can not live without him."

What would you have said if she had answered you thus? It certainly would not surprise me if you had been struck speechless. But if you were not and could still say something, you would undoubtedly have replied: "You misunderstand. I have not come to engage a hired girl. I am asking you to become my wife. I am not asking you for your assistance; I am asking you for your heart, as you have mine."

Whether any woman would give such a reply or not, I do not know. One hears many strange things these days. This I do know, that the Heavenly Bridegroom often receives such answers when He courts His poor and sinful earthly bride.

Many answer Him: "Yes, I will serve you. I will go to church; I will attend the Lord's Supper; I will read the Bible; I will pray daily; and I will participate in Christian work. I will honestly do all these things and do them as well as I can. But—you must excuse me —I love the world. And I can not think of living without permission to love it. But do not let that worry you. I will not be remiss in anything that you want done. And if I should ever forget anything, just call my attention to it, and I will at once apply myself with greater diligence to the exercise of my religious duties."

Thus they answer Him, generation after generation, daughter after mother, and son after father. And, to climax it all, they think that this is a "reasonable" service, in contradistinction to that of the pietists and enthusiasts, who, they say, always overdo things and go to extremes in religion.

The Heavenly Bridegroom has never asked you for moral offerings or religious service; He has not asked you for your prayers or your presence at the Lord's Supper or your participation in other ceremonials. He has asked you for this one thing: "My son, give me thy heart" (Proverbs 23:26).

This is the profound meaning of repentance. This is the logic of Christian conversion. This is the rationale of Christian worship. If God can not have our heart, He cares not at all for our religious ceremonials or our forced audiences with Him in church on Sunday morning or in our secret chamber. But if He gets possession of our heart, He gets everything else also. Then whatever we do for Him or our fellow-men is acceptable, because then it is done freely, out of love and gratitude.

*

When a man realizes that to repent means to yield his heart to God, then he is spiritually awake. And when he has been convinced that repentance means a change of heart, he has been projected into the greatest conflict which a man can experience.

It is more difficult to change one's heart than anything else. One may observe a marked change in one's outward life. One may pray and read the Bible each day, and struggle earnestly against one's old sinful habits. And even though one does not fully overcome them, nevertheless, a marked change will result. Others will notice it also. They may see such a great change in a man that they think he has been converted and treat him accordingly. This pleases him. He even feels good when old friends or acquaintances poke fun at him a little because of his godliness. It, too, indicates to him that a change of some kind must have taken place in his life.

But the hardest thing to change is his heart.

He prays every day, but, to be honest, he has to admit that he has no desire to do so. He also reads the Bible every day, but he has no desire for that either. He must force himself to do it. He likes to read the newspaper which lies beside the Bible. He reaches for it eagerly and reads it through every day. It interests him. But when he reads the Bible, he is often so absent in spirit that he reads along without really knowing what he is reading. He knows why: His heart is not in it.

He struggles against his sins every day. But, to be honest, he must admit that his love of sin is just as great as it ever was. In fact, he often wonders if his love of sin is not even greater than it was before his awakening.

He sees with disconcerting clearness that his attitude is unchanged, that his heart is not in his religion.

At first he is deeply and painfully grieved because of his sinful life and corrupt mind. Gradually, however, this fades away. He begins to look upon the whole affair with the attitude of a cold, indifferent spectator. He sees how corrupt and sinful he is, but it does not affect him. He has become hard-hearted and unemotional, very much as he was before he was awakened.

Besides, he has a feeling now which he can not recall ever having had before during his life as a worldling. He feels a spirit of opposition amounting almost to rebellion against God, because God has apparently made the way of salvation too narrow and untraversable for frail mankind. This rebelliousness is due to the fact that the man is now inwardly convinced that God is absolutely right when He demands a changed mind, when He asks for the heart, and declines to accept a heartless religiosity. At the same time this man is convinced of the fact that he can not change his heart. He can neither make himself hate sin nor love God.

This makes him think that God is unreasonable; His requirements are such that it is impossible for any human being to fulfill them.

This is one of Christianity's great paradoxes, one which the casual onlooker scarcely notices, but which plunges the earnest, awakened soul into despair. He feels in his conscience that God can not lower His requirements one jot; and, at the same time, he also feels that it is absolutely impossible for him to comply with them.

The earnest soul then asks in despair: How can I be converted? This I shall now try to answer.

First, however, I would like to tell you what conversion is not. So great is the misunderstanding at this point that I deem it necessary to clarify things a little more.

A person can not convert himself, can not by the sheer force of his own will cut himself loose from his former life and his old sins. He who tells us to repent knows that we are slaves of sin (John 8:34) and that we are sold under sin (Romans 7:14). He knows that not even by the strongest exercise of will-power is it possible for us to rid ourselves of our sin. This He alone can do who is the Saviour of sinners. That is why He said in the first sermon He preached in His home town: "The Spirit of the Lord is upon me, because He anointed me to . . . release the captives, and set at liberty them that are bruised" (Luke 4:18). To repent, therefore, you, a captive of sin, need only turn to Christ, reach out your shackled hands and feet to Him and say: "Lord, I shall never be released unless Thou dost release me from my sins."

Whether you are held captive by open sins and everybody around you knows of your shame, or you are held by secret sins and only God and you know how sin has disgraced and humiliated you, He alone has the power to release you from the bonds of sin. He is the only one who can set at liberty the sin-bound slave and pour consolation into the troubled heart.

To repent is not to press forth by your own will-power a hatred of sin and a love of God. He who admonishes us to repent knows that this can not be done "by the will of the flesh, nor of the will of man, but of God" (John 1:1-3).

No sinful man can of himself bring forth a true change of heart. God must do that. We have spoken of this in a previous chapter where we dealt with the mysterious element in Christianity. God must by the miracle of regeneration bring forth in the sinner that new heart which loves God and abhors sin.

*

But then some one asks: What part does man have in bringing about this change of mind? Is it not we who are admonished to turn about and repent?

After what I have already said, this is comparatively easy to answer. We sinful men can not change our own hearts, begin to love God, and hate sin. What we have to do in conversion is something entirely different and exceedingly much more simple.

It is this: When the Spirit of God begins to convict us of sin, we are simply to permit ourselves to be convicted, and to acknowledge the truth of what the Spirit says concerning our outward life as well as our heart. When this is done, a great change has taken place in our hearts, a change which is a result of our own choice.

Formerly we would not permit ourselves to be convicted by the Spirit of God. We sought rather to avoid every serious reminder of sin in our consciences. *Now* we turn to God and tell Him the whole truth where we *formerly* tried to conceal ourselves from Him. *Now* we desire to be reconciled to God and have even the smallest sin forgiven; formerly we tried to avoid reconciliation, or else tried to compromise with God and our own consciences and get away as easily as possible.

What a change of heart!

Here comes the sinner, formerly thoughtless and frivolous or self-satisfied, now humiliated and crushed by the truth, poor and helpless. Behind him towers his sinful life, heaven-high in its accusations against him. Within him is a heart filled to overflowing with sin, a heart which loves sin and not God. And, worst of all, he is unable in his own strength to change this heart of his.

Here he comes, wavering, groping, shy and fearful, because he feels that he can not come to God in this condition. But Jesus beckons to him and says in His friendly way: "him that cometh to me I will in no wise cast out" (John 6:37). Then the sinner takes courage and goes directly to the Saviour with all his sinfulness.

He is saved.

For now, since Christ has died for sin, a sinner need do nothing more to be saved than to conceal or spare no sin, but lay everything before the Saviour. "If we confess our sins, He is faithful and righteous to forgive us our sins, and to cleanse us from all unrighteousness" (I. John 1:9). "But He was wounded for our transgressions, He was bruised for our iniquities; the chastisement of our peace was upon Him; and with His stripes we are healed" (Isaiah 53:5).

BOOK SIX

The Choice

"Enter ye in by the narrow gate: for wide is the gate, and broad is the way that leadeth to destruction."—Matthew 7:13.

"No man can serve two masters."—Matthew 6:24.

"Whosoever therefore would be a friend of the world maketh himself an enemy of God."—James 4:4.

A S I observe the people I meet, I notice that there are two distinct classes who have made a definite choice of the course they are pursuing in life.

They are the avowed believers and the avowed ungodly.

Both of these classes live a life which shows that they have made a clear and definite choice.

But between these two groups is that great mass of human beings which has made no choice, which does not will to make any, and which is even afraid to choose.

It does not surprise me that they are afraid.

Everybody has a native fear of a great and decisive choice, that is, a choice which involves many and far-reaching consequences. There is something within us which seeks to avoid all choosing. We do not care to burn the bridges behind us. We want a way open for retreat in case too many difficulties should arise.

This fear naturally becomes doubly great when a person is confronted with the most decisive choice of all in life:

139

the choice of one's relationship to God. There are numerous decisions in a person's life which entail many and far-reaching consequences. There is, for instance, the relationship in which a child chooses to stand toward its parents. The old Mosaic words: "Honor thy father and thy mother, that it may be well with thee, and thou mayest live long on the earth," are an eternal law for mankind, which no child can violate and go unpunished. The attitude which a man chooses to take toward the law of the land is also a decisive factor in his life.

But the relationship in which a person chooses to stand toward God is, without comparison, the most important of all. This is because of the simple fact that God is God.

Because this choice is the most important of all, it is feared more than any other; and for that reason people try to avoid it.

These people who live midway between the avowed believers and the avowed ungodly think, as a rule, that it is not necessary to make any choice.

They do not desire by any means to break with God. Their life is woven together with God in such an intimate way that life apart from Him is unthinkable.

In the first place, they are, like all other people, religious. They have within themselves a hidden longing for eternal things, a secret attraction toward the source of their being. A capacity for God, a desire for God, lies deeply imbedded in all of us.

When our soul left the hand of God, our creator, He put His stamp upon it and marked it for His own. This mark of ownership can not be removed by any one, either in time or in eternity. Even if a person loses his soul, becomes eternally lost, he can not escape consciousness of the fact that his soul is God's rightful possession.

There are some men, it is true, who maintain that they are not religious. And I do not doubt their sincerity. But I do doubt whether they understand themselves.

All people are religious by nature. The history of religion shows us that plainly. There is not a people on earth without a religion. A generation ago anti-Christian and atheistic scientists tried to prove that there were races that had no religion. They reported that they had found a primitive people in central Africa that had absolutely no religion. However, the exultation of these scientists was very short lived, because it was based upon consummate ignorance of some of the most elementary phases of religious life. An investigation by experts showed that this people had a mystery religion, which they tried as hard as they could to conceal from the uninitiated.

Lack of religion is, in other words, not a natural but an artificial product. It is brought into existence when the innate tendencies in human life toward religion are deliberately undernourished and suppressed, when people make themselves believe by the exercise of "reason" that there can be no objective reality corresponding to their subjective longings and ideas about an invisible world and an invisible Supreme Being back of the world of phenomena.

In fact, the extreme religiosity of the human soul never becomes more apparent, perhaps, than in these very people who profess to have no religion. Their fight against religion is usually waged in such a way that it becomes very evident that their real battle is against the religiosity of their own soul. In spite of their deliberate suppression of the divine yearnings of their soul, their religiosity often breaks through, especially when they come to close grips with the deep problems of life and their soul-life is allowed to express itself untrammeled by reflection and prejudice.

Some time ago in one of the countries of northern Europe a man died who had been a leader in the cultural life of the nation. He lived as an atheist and died as such. But after his death a few small slips of paper were found scattered throughout his otherwise well arranged posthumous papers. On these slips of paper he had from time to time committed to writing the distressing cries of his soul to the God whom he had persistently denied.

Verily, the soul of man is religious!

God has, however, not only endowed us with religious capacities and longings. He satisfies those longings. We were baptized as babes. At that time He met our soul's religious needs, and that even before we had asked Him to do so. Such is God.

In a mystical, wonderful way He planted the deepest and finest roots of our being deep down into His own being. We received life in God in a wonderful way. During the first two or three years we lived a quiet life as God's children, under the constant influence of the living God, undisturbed by our surroundings.

As self-consciousness began to develop, we met earth's most beautiful revelation of the love of God in our dear mother. There is none like mother, so tender and mild, so beautiful and good. No one understands like mother. No one forgives like mother. No one is as patient as mother.

And never was mother more dear than when she lifted her little one into her lap at eventide and began to tell about Jesus. Those were the best hours we experienced. She told us the story so gently and so simply. Everything was so real and came so close to us. It seemed as though Jesus was walking about in the room.

In this way Jesus entered quietly into our little daily life and knit our soul to Himself by a thousand strands of gold.

Then came the happiest day of all the year, Christmas Eve, with Christmas trees, Christmas candles, Christmas joy, and Christmas gifts. When the lights had been lit and all had been seated about the table, father stepped solemnly over to the bookshelf, took down the big, old Book, sat down, and read the most wonderful story of all that can be read here on earth. I imagine that you can still feel a little of that which passed through your soul and body as the impressive words penetrated the stillness: "And it came to pass in those days, there went out a decree from Caesar Augustus, that all the world should be enrolled . . . "

Time passed.

The day came when you were to start school. Mother accompanied you, and you went with many a strange and anxious thought. But your teacher was kind and good, and you began to like her from the start. At first you were always well-behaved and industrious. Later on you became a little naughty perhaps, at least occasionally. Not so, however, during the period of religious instruction. It was different from all the other classes.[1] There you could not be unruly, because the teacher spoke of Jesus in such a way that you often felt as though He were present in the room. Your heart was softened, and you repented bitterly of the evil you had done.

Again time passed.

You enrolled in the pastor's confirmation class. You

---

[1]Christian instruction is given in the public schools of Norway.

were perhaps fortunate enough to have a pastor who knew how to speak to your young heart. When he spoke, it seemed as though God drew very near to you. You experienced a great deal during those months of preparation for confirmation.

Your confirmation day came. You were to stand before God and the congregation and witness the good confession. I do not know how you felt that day. I do know that to me it was a day full of seriousness and earnestness. I desired to "renounce the devil and all his works and all his ways." I believed in the Triune God. Such was most likely also the case with you.

Soon afterwards came your first communion. That moved you even more. You stood in the presence of the greatest mystery given to man on earth. You wept like a child, and scarcely knew what was happening as you accompanied your father and mother up to the altar to receive the sacrament of the body and blood of our Lord.

How true it is that God enters our life by many various pathways, and binds our soul to Himself by many tender bonds!

Time passed again.

Life is many-sided. It is not all sunshine and play. Dark, heavy shadows began to descend upon your home. Was it father who became ill? How everything was changed! Father was so quiet during his illness. You all became very quiet, too. He wanted you to read and sing for him often. You heard him pray to God. As a rule he said very little. But now and then he would say a few words to you about God, words which went to the very marrow of your bones. At such times he would weep, and you would weep, too. But it was all so quiet and peaceful.

One day the pastor was summoned. Father desired to partake of Holy Communion. You no doubt remember what a solemn hour it was. The room had been given a festive touch. Father lay happy and full of anticipation. Soon the venerable servant of the Lord came with the holy sacrament. An atmosphere of assurance and peace was noticeable even before he began to speak. You sat and looked at your father all the time. When he had participated in the sacred repast in preparation for the long journey, his countenance beamed with inexpressible and glorified joy. Deep down in your heart you thanked God because He can thus refresh and strengthen a soul in the midst of the terrible death-struggle.

Then father died. A few days afterward his dear body was lowered into the depths of the grave. Then, too, God drew near unto you in your sorrow, and spoke these mighty words: "Blessed be God who hath begotten us again unto a lively hope by the resurrection of Jesus Christ from the dead." He told you that you would see your father again on that great resurrection morn when all who are in the graves shall hear the voice of the Son of God, and they shall come forth who have done good unto the resurrection of life.

Time passed again.

You were engaged to be married. At last your wedding day came. God was with you and made the day the happiest one in your life. He met you at the altar, and promised you that if you would open your hearts and home to Him, He would make all the bright and beautiful dreams come true which you had dreamed about your home and wedded life.

The following year you were given your first-born. Great was your joy. Again God entered quietly into the midst of your happiness. Soon the little one was to be baptized. I presume you felt as I did when we brought our first-born to the baptismal font. It was as if God said to me: "Now the little one is not yours alone any longer; he is mine also. You love him, but I love him even more. Together we shall now in love guide him into a good and happy life and into the very kingdom of heaven itself."

On the way home from church I felt as though we had received the little one as a gift from God a second time.

*

This and a great deal more we all experience. Some of my readers have already experienced it. Others have experienced only a part of it. And it is only a matter of time, perhaps, and they will experience the remainder.

Thus God weaves Himself quietly and tenderly into human life. He knits by a thousand strands the finest and deepest life of the soul to the living God. Every festive and solemn occasion in the inner as well as the outward life of such a person has been blessed by God.

It is therefore inconceivable for these people to think of breaking with God and living without Him. They desire to keep up their connection with the God of their fathers and of their own childhood.

They go to church, occasionally also to the Lord's Table. They are, as a rule, very much interested in questions pertaining to the church and to Christianity. They are generous towards the poor and liberal givers to the various branches of Christian work. They are numbered among the pastor's most faithful supporters in the congregation; he never appeals to them in vain.

*

Such are the people who live midway between the

avowed believers and the avowedly ungodly, and who seek to avoid making the great and decisive choice.

That is the way they appear from one side.

But they have another side, too.

This side is not so bright, and therefore not so easy to speak about. But if I am to be faithful to the truth, I must say a few words about this side also.

They love the world.

That is what the Bible says about every life which will not permit itself to be directed by God. These people love worldliness and can not think of living without it. They love an easy, comfortable life, and seek to avoid as far as possible all serious and heart-searching questions. Regard for personal advantage, personal honor, and, in doubtful instances, what others might say, are the determining factors in their life, both at home as well as away from home. They do not look to God or their own conscience for guidance, but do as the majority does.

They love that worldly life in which people help each other to pamper their flesh in refined and respectable ways, by means of entertainments, amusements, society life, and a social life in general in which the truth both in word and in deed is carefully suppressed, according to a general agreement known as "good etiquette."

No open ungodliness is allowed, no excesses of any kind. Everything is respectable and proper. They are good, honorable, capable people, an asset to their own home as well as to the community at large.

But they bend their energies and their goodness toward this one goal: to unite God and worldliness. They try to maintain a balance whereby they need neither to break with God nor offend the world. Not more worldly than that they can associate respectably with the pastor and the church, and not more Christian than "good etiquette" will permit.

*

Then comes Jesus with His mighty and inexorable: "either-or." "Enter ye in by the narrow gate: for wide is the gate, and broad is the way, that leadeth to destruction, and many are they that enter in thereby." "No man can serve two masters." "Whosoever therefore would be a friend of the world maketh himself an enemy of God."

It is Jesus who has put this "either-or" into life.

He has drawn the real line of demarcation between people. We, too, distinguish between people in various ways. We divide them into the rich and the poor, according to the amount of money they have. We classify them as educated or uneducated, according to the knowledge they have acquired. And we look upon them as cultured or uncouth, often according to the clothes they wear.

But neither clothes nor wealth nor knowledge constitute a real basis for classifying people.

Jesus has pointed out the real difference between them. The old prophet foretold it as early as the time of the Saviour's birth: "Behold, this child is set for the *falling* and *rising* of many in Israel" (Luke 2:34). Which is exactly what happened. He went through the nation and divided it into two groups: those who heard Him unto salvation and those who were offended in Him and thus lost. In like manner Jesus has passed through mankind down through the centuries, and has divided men into two classes: those who chose to follow Him and those who chose to reject Him.

They may otherwise be as closely bound together by ties of blood and friendship as it is possible for men to be: parents and children, brothers and sisters, husband and wife, friends and comrades. When Jesus comes, He sets up an inner wall of separation between those who humble themselves before Him and those who reject Him. Even though they work together side by side every day, eat at the same table, or lie in the same bed, nevertheless, their lives are separated by a great gulf.

The different attitudes which men take toward Jesus is the real mark of separation between them. This separation is also to be an eternal one, Jesus says. On the great day at the end of time this separation will become openly and irrevocably manifest. Jesus Himself portrays this in the judgment scene (Matthew 25:31-46): As the shepherd divides the sheep from the goats, so shall He separate the human race forever into two groups: those who accepted the Saviour and those who rejected Him. "And these shall go away into eternal punishment, but the righteous into eternal life."

Scarcely any other passage in the Gospels shows us more clearly how conscious Jesus was of putting the eternal and inexorable "either-or" into human life. He is the rock in the midst of the stream of life by which the human race is to be divided into two classes.

*

Jesus puts this "either-or" before the individual also. And He does so without asking our permission. He compels no one; all of us are at liberty to choose the attitude we wish to take toward Him. But He sees to it that we are brought face to face with Him. He does not ask our permission for that, either. He sees to it that no man is permitted to walk the broad way to eternal perdition without first having been confronted with his only Saviour.

It appears to us often as though men pursue their unsaved course fairly undisturbed. They seem to sin thoughtlessly and carelessly, without even a thought of sin or punishment, soul or conscience, death or judgment, God or eternity. But, God be praised, such is not the case.

I remember an incident from my childhood days which even now speaks to my heart. We were a group of lively boys, and we did a number of things which deserved punishment. But father was busy outside the home, and he could not always attend to these things every time it became necessary.

But at times father would come in and punish the young offender. I shall never forget those times no matter how old I become. He came in such a quiet, kindly way. He was so irresistibly kind. He would take the little offender up into his lap, and there I would sit wriggling like a worm. It was so unbearable to look into father's kind, grieved, tear-filled eyes. For now I had to look him in the eye.

That is also the way of Him who is the Father of all that bear the name child in heaven and on earth. He suffers His children to sin for a long time and to despise His love. But the day finally comes—for which everything has been made ready. He summons the transgressor into His presence and says: "I must have a word with you before you proceed any farther upon your unsaved way."

That person has not been born who must not at such a time stop and listen. Everything quakes beneath one's feet. Confronted with the living God, the sinner becomes filled with holy anxiety. His soul trembles with unspeakable fear and terror. A blazing light is focused upon his sinfulness. Old sins and new rise accusingly against him, like a mountain of indictments which threatens to fall upon him and crush him. Sins long since forgotten come to light again and pain the soul like an open, smarting sore.

At such times, however, a person does not only see his sins; he also sees his Saviour. To a thoughtless person that is almost worse than to see his sins. He now learns to know what Jesus is like. Up to this time he has not known Him very well. He has gone through life with the ordinary caricature of Jesus impressed upon his superficial soul. He has thought of God as a strict Lord, Who was hard to deal with and Who understood and cared little about human misery or happiness. He would, perhaps, even prefer to deprive men of whatever joy they might be able to wrest from their brief and weary sojourn in this life. And finally cast them into everlasting torment in case they did not comply with His strict requirements concerning repentance and regeneration, and many other things which are both unreasonable and impossible to understand.

The sinner is now permitted to "see" his Saviour. He sees that Jesus is neither hard nor gruesome nor unreasonable. Wounded and bleeding, the Saviour approaches the human offender, not to scare, nor to scold, and still less to torment and destroy. He comes to you. He comes because He can not endure to see you waste your brief years in sin and lose your immortal soul. He comes to tell you where it will all end if you continue. And He tells you that He can save you and transform your life into a new, rich, and happy one, if you will but admit Him into your life.

The hardest thing for you, however, is to look into the eyes of Jesus. He does not speak a harsh or reproachful word to you, but sees, of course, your inner distress. And every time you are almost persuaded but fail to follow His urgent call and your own conviction, you see his tear-filled eyes resting solemnly upon you.

Verily, the love of Christ is the hardest thing for that sinner to face who clings to sin and will not choose Christ. From that day sin is no longer a pleasure. Sin becomes harsh and bitter. Henceforth it feels like going to one's own execution whenever one permits oneself to be drawn away into the old life and into the old companionships.

*

Such a soul is confronted with the choice.

It is absolutely clear to him now that it is impossible to unite God and worldliness. It is clear that it is not enough to be somewhat religious; that no one is saved merely by seeking God; that no one can enter into the kingdom of heaven merely by circling around outside of the narrow gate. One must enter *in through* the narrow gate. He sees now that Jesus is right: "No man can serve two masters." "Whosoever would be a friend of the world maketh himself an enemy of God."

He sees it now: A person becomes a Christian, not by longing, nor by hoping, nor by waiting, nor by thinking, nor by talking, nor by sighing, nor by weeping. Nay, a choice must be made. It becomes evident that the course he is now pursuing will never lead him to the desired goal. He must decide whom to follow: God or the world.

But this is also what is hardest for that person.

What shall he choose?

If he chooses God, the world will turn against him. If he chooses the world, he will have to break with God. Both are equally hard. To break with God is impossible! And the thought of incurring the disfavor of the world, of

facing its cynical smiles, mockery, its condescending sym-
pathy, is equally intolerable.

In such a time a person weeps many bitter tears.

*

There is also something almost exasperating about this.
How can a mere choice entail consequences as high as the
heavens and as far-reaching as eternity? One moment
an unsaved soul; the next, saved. Merely by a choice!

I admit willingly that this is remarkable. But it is true,
nevertheless. May I at this point underline this remarkable aspect of the choice in connection with repentance?

First, let me point out that this choice, like all other
choices, involves but a moment's time. This lies in the
very nature of a choice and can not be otherwise. I may
deliberate upon and consider a choice for years. The
actual choosing, however, is not a matter of two moments
but one.

This moment's choice results in an epoch-making change
in my life, both for time and for eternity! That this is
remarkable can not be denied. At one moment I am an
unsaved soul; in the next, saved. At one moment I am
a debt-laden soul, temporally and eternally; in the next,
entirely free from guilt. At one moment I am, according
to the Scripture, a child of the devil; in the next, a child
of God. At one moment I am walking the broad way to
perdition; in the next, standing in the midst of the narrow gate on the narrow way which leads to the fair
homeland of heaven.

How can such truly great and remarkable things follow as the result of a mere choice?

Permit me first to answer thus: This is not due to the
choice in itself. And for that reason it does not depend
upon the clarity of your thought, the intensity of your

feelings, or the exertion of your will while making the choice. Nay, the saving virtue of the choice is due to something else entirely. The saving virtue lies in the new relationship to your one and only Saviour, Jesus Christ, into which your choice has brought you.

Jesus says: "Behold, I stand at the door and knock: if any man hear my voice and open the door, I will come in to him and sup with him, and he with me" (Revelation 3:20).

The saving virtue of the choice lies in this, that you choose to open your soul to Jesus and let Him enter with all His saving power and do the work which He, better than any one else, can do in a sin-laden and sin-burdened soul.

Notice now the necessity of the choice.

Jesus stands at the door and knocks; that is, He makes it known that He desires admittance. What do men do when Jesus knocks? They do one of three things.

They may listen with indifference and obstinacy to His earnest and tender call.—And in case their hearts become too restless, they try to drown out the knocking at their heart's door in the noise and tumult of which a worldly life is so full.

Or, they go to the door, open it slightly, and begin to negotiate for peace with Jesus. Their hearts are so restless and full of misery that they know there must be a change. They must have peace with God. But they want it at the lowest possible price. Consequently, they try to negotiate, to make a bargain with our Lord. They desire to be saved, and they sigh and cry and yearn very fervently for it. But they tell the Lord on what conditions. They want to be saved without repentance. They want to be saved, but without breaking unconditionally with sin and their worldly life. They want to be saved, but without yielding themselves unreservedly and giving Him full sway.

Many stop here. Especially in our religious age. People are satisfied with seeking God instead of pressing on through the narrow gate and finding God. The little religious awakening which they have experienced and which nowadays is elegantly styled "religious experience," they use as a cloak every time the Holy Spirit of God through their conscience demands a genuine conversion.

Or, thirdly, they do exactly as Jesus asks them to do. They open the door to Him that He may enter in. *In that moment that soul is converted.*

What takes place at that moment is this: That soul chooses to stand in an entirely new relationship to Christ. One no longer tries to drown out His knocking at the heart's door. One no longer tries to negotiate a compromise with Jesus. The soul has chosen to open the door, that is, to surrender to God without dissimulation, without artifice, without conditions, and without delay.

People speak of a converted person as *one who has surrendered to God*. It is an excellent expression, perhaps the best expression we have for characterizing the quintessence of conversion.

What does it mean to surrender?

We know that from the war. He who surrenders, first lays down his arms and then throws up his empty hands to let his foe know that he will no longer use weapons against him. He delivers himself up disarmed, asks no terms, and thrusts himself upon the mercy of the other.

That is what takes place when a person is converted.

He first lays down all the weapons he has used against

God and his own conscience. He then surrenders himself to God's merciful dealings, without naming any conditions or making any demands.

The paths are now open into the very innermost recesses of his soul. He does not try to hide any of his sins. Everything, old sins and new, small sins and great, is candidly and unsparingly acknowledged before God. The sinner desires to spare no sin nor smuggle any into the new life of fellowship with God. Everything to the light! All relationships, all habits are laid openly before God in order that He may decide whether they are sinful or not.

It is easier now to say how the choice of one moment can entail such enormous consequences.

Because Jesus has died for our sins, nothing more is necessary on our part in order to be saved than this one thing: not to refuse Jesus admittance, but to open our heart to Him when He comes to us with His great salvation and knocks at the door for the purpose of making us partakers in it. He enters and begins to sup with our soul, according to His promise in Revelation 3:20.

In the first place, He gives us full remission of sin, which He has won for us by His own precious blood. Then He gives us new life by His Spirit. A holy life, which manifests itself in hunger and thirst after righteousness, in smarting pain and grief at offending God, in an inner sense of impotence with respect to sin, which draws the soul to the cross and to the heart of Jesus, and in a constant feeling of our inability to do good, which gives the soul no peace except when beholding Jesus. And, finally, He gives us peace and joy in our hearts, as much as is compatible with our spiritual development and growth in grace.

Some of my readers are perhaps saying to themselves: "This applies to me. I have always avoided the choice. But I have for some time been aware that I must choose. My soul is longing, yea, crying out for peace with God. Now and then at least. But I can not. I dare not. What would my friends and acquaintances say if they were to hear that I was converted? The mere thought of their smiles of derision and their commiseration is enough to frighten me."

Indeed, my friend, we are cowards. Cowardice is one of our lowest and vilest traits. There is scarcely anything which shows us more clearly how sin has destroyed our soul-life. It is terrible that man can forget God, his Creator and Father. Still worse that he transgresses His will and resists Him. But worst of all, it seems to me, is this, that man is ashamed of God, even when he is convicted of sin and knows that he can not be saved except by surrendering to God. Then not to dare to do so because it is a shame to be a true Christian!

To be a half Christian is not looked upon as a shame; on the contrary, it is considered quite compatible with the highest degree of culture. But to be a whole-hearted Christian, one who gives heed to God and not to man, is considered uncultured. How the truth has been perverted in our enlightened and cultured age!

People are not ashamed to swear and curse. Nowadays even women take the name of God in vain and know full well that they are not committing a breach of "good etiquette." But to mention the name of God seriously and lovingly, of this they are ashamed. There are without a question not a few people who would rather be looked upon as scoundrels than to be known as living Christians.

What good does this do me, you ask. I am a big coward. Tell me if there is any hope for a man like me.

My friend, I am glad to offer you a Gospel which holds out hope for all who will honestly come to Christ. There is only one class of people which Christ can not help. It is those who are not sincere when they come to Him.

Let me tell you that I was just as much of a coward as you. Perhaps that might give you a little help and encouragement. We are all cowards. Jesus knows us. And He is not surprised at our cowardice. He is prepared for it. He does not expect either you or me to have courage of ourselves to break with the world and surrender to God.

One thing, however, He does expect: that we come to Him and tell Him honestly how cowardly we are. And ask Him to give us the courage we lack. Do this and you will see what Christ can do for you. All who have been saved so far have been thus helped. That is the way He helped me, too. It was as if He said to me: "Now put your trembling little hand in mine, and together we two will go to the people you fear so much."

And I went with Him. And all went well. Some of my friends began to cry when I began to tell them what God had done for me. Others listened to me patiently and said when I was through: "Well, just stick to it." Others, again, looked upon the whole thing with a skeptical smile. But that, too, could be borne.

*

I can imagine that here and there among my readers are some who are saying: "This does not apply particularly to me. I am past this. Fear of men no longer keeps me from making the decisive choice which I know I should make. Conditions in my home are what hinder me.

We get along so well in our home. True, neither of us is perfect, but we live together beautifully and harmoniously. We share everything and are very intimately attached to each other.

If I should become a true Christian, what would become of our home? It would be ruined. Our mutual confidence would come to an end, because we would no longer be sharing the same views with respect to life's most important questions. By my new life I would bring discord into our idyllic little home. And I do not know what that might lead to. Perhaps our little home would be broken up, because my husband could not endure to have me live the richest and deepest part of my life apart from him. Might there not also be a danger that I might drive him farther away from God and even, perhaps, make it impossible for him to be saved? He might become so bitter toward God and Christianity that it would harden his heart completely."

In reply to this I would say first: I understand well your thoughts and your fears. A good home is certainly worth preserving by all the means which can stand the test of the light of God. God bless both you and your good home. Might we have many such homes among our beloved people!

But then I must also tell you what Jesus says in this connection: "He that loveth father and mother more than me is not worthy of me" (Matthew 10:37). I know that deep down in your heart there is something which tells you that Jesus is right. You should not be compelled to ask any person, not even those nearest to you, for permission to be in the right relationship to your

Saviour. Any one who demands that you act according to his and not your own conscience in this matter does not truly love you.

Furthermore, I have something else to tell you: "Believe on the Lord Jesus, and thou shalt be saved, *thou and thy house*" (Acts 16:31). You and your house shall be saved; this is the promise of the Lord. How is this to take place? When you believe on the Lord Jesus, that is, surrender to Him without taking counsel with flesh and blood. You will be saved first. And through you the rest will be won also.

The Lord would like to enter your home. He has been knocking a long time already. He must gain entrance now through you. If you for the sake of peace in the family do not dare to take the step, perhaps your idyllic home life will come to an end with you two going arm in arm to eternal perdition. But if you repent now, you will be able to help your loved ones into life in God. Then your home will afford you an even deeper and purer joy than you have heretofore had.

Assume bravely the trials and difficulties which you will encounter at first, until you have won your loved ones. The Lord will be with you each day with His invisible power and guide you in all your ways.

Furthermore, it is by no means certain that you will encounter as much opposition as you beforehand fear you will. Many married folk have been happily surprised, when one finally confided to the other that he or she had been converted, to hear the other reply immediately by saying: "God be praised that such is the case with you, too. I have had this in mind for a long time, but I have been uncertain as to how you would take it. And for that reason I have not been able to make myself say anything to you about it."

*

Gracious God! I thank Thee that I have made the choice. And I thank Thee for each step I have been permitted to take upon the narrow way in Thy footsteps. I thank Thee for the blessed joy of being a Christian. I pray Thee for those who have not made the choice, and who stand fearful and anxious before the narrow gate of decision. Thou who didst help me to choose, help them also. Especially those who feel in their conscience that they ought to make the choice now. Give them a vision of Thee, Lord, that they hesitate no longer, but cast themselves forthwith into Thy pierced hands. Amen.

BOOK SEVEN

To Those Who Have Chosen

BEFORE I bring this book to a close, I should like to speak a few words to you who have made the choice.

The period immediately following the choice is as a rule not an easy one. Everything is new and strange. There is no previous experience to be guided by. One's preconceived ideas and expectations as to how it all would be, are usually found to be wrong. Great surprises and disappointments are the result. Often one feels completely disorientated and at a loss as to what to do.

One is like a newly planted tree which has not as yet struck root in its new surroundings. One has very little poise and consequently low powers of resistance. The least pressure from without seems to upset everything. Inwardly one is often helplessly subject to one's emotions. To fall or to suffer defeat brings remorse almost to the point of despair. One feels that such sin can not be forgiven, that he can not come back and ask forgiveness after having been untrue to a loving Saviour.

At other times one may be entirely emotionless. One's despair at this is just as great. Everything seems to be gone. One feels that he has dealt so carelessly with that which God has wrought in his soul that there is nothing left of it. The Lord seems to have withdrawn Himself. He does not care any longer for one who has been so indifferent with regard to the salvation of his soul.

At such times one is also tempted to believe that the whole thing was a product of the imagination, a beautiful illusion, which went to pieces the first time it came in contact with the stern realities of life. Was it anything but emotional intoxication? As long as it lasted I naively believed that it was the work of God. Now it is all too apparent that I was a victim of self-deception. In despair one says to himself: "If this *was* not conversion, then it is absolutely impossible for me to be truly converted. Since this happens every time I try, it must be because I am not sincere enough in my determination to be saved."

There is also another difficulty. Some attain a state of wonderful bliss, and that at the very moment when they surrender to God, while others experience no such joy and peace at first. On the contrary, for them it becomes a very strenuous and restless period. And some feel as though all the powers of evil have been turned loose upon them from the day they chose to surrender to God.

In the first place, one's conscience is often so tender and sore that it is almost impossible to say or do anything without feeling a sting of reproach afterwards. Such anxiety often follows these reproaches of conscience that one scarcely knows what to do with oneself. Such people feel as though they are sinning knowingly and deliberately and that the wrath of God abides upon them day and night. It is, therefore, easy for them to give up all hope and think that they are worse than everybody else and that they have undoubtedly reached the stage where it is impossible to be saved.

Others have the experience immediately after their conversion that sin tempts them as never before. Not only do the old, sinful habits tempt them worse than ever, but sins which are comparatively new present themselves with an alluring appeal. These people feel at times as though there is scarcely a sin but what they lust after it. And the only reason they do not commit it is that they are afraid of the consequences.

These people ask themselves in bewilderment and despair: What has happened to me? I thought that I had been converted to God. And I did it to get away from my old life in sin. But I am worse than I ever was. There must be something wrong with my conversion. I suppose I have grieved the Holy Spirit of God and that He has forsaken me because I am so completely dominated by the might and power of sin.

*

Those people, too, who at the time of their conversion were filled with joy and peace, will, after a while, and as a rule very soon, get into deep water and encounter difficulties of various kinds. Very often they have the experience of losing their joy. This leaves them with an uncomfortable vacuum in their hearts. With the loss of their joy they feel that God, too, has forsaken them. They say with weeping Mary Magdalene at the grave of Jesus: "They have taken away my Lord, and I know not where they have laid Him" (John 20:13).

Occasionally the blissful emotions return for a season, and grief is dispelled for the time being. Such vacillation between sunshine and shadow occurs very frequently during this early period. And it is the cause of a great deal of pain and anxiety.

But worse than this, at times such souls feel that their whole new blessed life is beginning to ebb away. Not only do their periods of joy become briefer and occur with less frequency as time passes, but they notice that everything pertaining to godliness in their life is quietly fading away.

The Bible, which formerly was such a precious book, has gradually become more and more burdensome to read. Secret prayer, which formerly was such a great joy, has gradually become a burden. To hear the word of God and to assemble with the people of God were the greatest of all joys. But this, too, has little by little lost its attractiveness. As a result they quietly stay away from as many meetings as they respectably can, and force themselves to attend the rest.

And sin, which they were able to withstand with such wonderful power during the first period of joy and happiness, has gradually begun to exercise its former sway again, not suddenly, but gradually and imperceptibly. Consequently they have not paid particular attention to it each time it happened, and as a result it has taken place without a great deal of opposition.

Now and then they wake up and see that things are going the wrong way. Then they put forth tremendous efforts, pray and read twice as much as before, and struggle hard against their sinful habits. But only for the time being. In a short time they are back in the old ruts again. Then they awaken anew out of their lethargy and exert themselves with much concern. They are firmly determined to work up within themselves once more, by faithful and diligent effort, the love for prayer and the Word of God and the hatred toward sin which they formerly had. But they do not succeed.

After vainly trying to make themselves believe that things are not very bad, or that they will gradually adjust themselves, they finally reach a point where they are compelled to acknowledge that they do not love God and do not hate sin. That is, it is clear that their conversion was a complete failure. Conversion is a change of heart, and that is precisely what has not taken place.

The question now arises as to whether the conversion they had experienced was a true conversion. Was it not rather what Jesus describes in the following words: "And he that was sown upon the rocky places, this is he that heareth the word, and *straightway with joy receiveth it; yet hath he not root in himself, but endureth for a while?*" (Matthew 13:20-21).

We comfort others with the same comfort wherewith we have been comforted, says the apostle. That is what I shall try to do in this connection.

First, let me remind you of what conversion really is. To be converted is not the same as to be sinless. Do not become confused and do not begin to despair when you discover that your old sinful nature is still active within you. Do not be frightened if you find that sin tempts you worse now than it did before. You are not the only one who has had that experience. The Apostle Paul felt it also: "When the commandment came, sin *revived*" (Romans 7:9).

To be converted is not to become sinless, but to take a new attitude toward sin: Whereas formerly I thwarted my own conscience and sinned deliberately, or else tried to evade the judgment of my conscience either by excusing my sin or making it appear laudable in some way, now I am determined to know the truth about myself and my sins. I pray the Spirit of God to show me the truth in such a way that I can not fail to understand it. Whenever I am convinced that something in my life is contrary to the will of God, I turn to the Saviour and tell it all to Him. I cling to the plain words of Scripture: "If we confess our sins, he is faithful and righteous to forgive us our sins, and to cleanse us from all unrighteousness" (I John 1:9).

Nor should you become confused in case you are overwhelmed with anxiety. It is easy for you to think that this is a sign that God will have nothing to do with you. You must not, however, let yourself be guided by your own thoughts or feelings. You can not rely upon them in this matter. Nay, search the Word of God and find out what God thinks of you. You will find some very plain statements: "Him that cometh to me I will in no wise cast out" (John 6:37). God loves you. Read again the beautiful description of the love of God which Jesus gives in the parable of the prodigal son in the fifteenth chapter of the Gospel according to Luke.

Yes, but why am I so fearful, you say, if God loves me?

Your fear is also proof that God loves you. It, too, is a result of the work of the Holy Spirit. It is not anxiety *unto God* which He is working within you. Herein you misunderstand Him. He is now making you anxious with respect to sin. Such anxiety is a precious gift from God, for which later on you will be very grateful, after you have had a little more experience.

This fear, then, is not proof that there is something wrong with your conversion, but, on the contrary, very definite proof that you have been converted and have

been given that truly repentant heart which fears God
and desires to do nothing against Him. In this connection, too, we have a decisive passage from Paul: "Work
out your own salvation with fear and trembling" (Philippians 2:12).

The fear which you are now experiencing is not abnor-
mal. It is part and parcel of the salvation which you are
experiencing. It has a double purpose. To help separate
you from sin and to keep you close to the Saviour. Its
purpose is to make you so dependent upon your merciful
and mighty Saviour that you can not live without Him
a single hour of the day.

Nor should you despair if you become the victim of a
surprise attack by your old sinful habits, causing you to
fall deeply and shamefully. It is very humiliating to
your own pride to suffer such defeats. And it is even
worse to remember that you are disappointing and griev-
ing God and bringing shame upon the Name by which
you are named.

I know that in such moments you are tempted to
give up everything. Nevertheless, go confidently to your
new Friend. He Himself says: "The Son of Man came
to seek and to save that which was *lost*" (Luke 19:10).
Listen again: "I came not to call the *righteous*, but
sinners" (Matthew 9:13). He also says, even more en-
couragingly: "They that are whole have no need of a
physician, but they that are sick" (Matthew 9:12).
Whenever you err, you know what you should do: let
yourself be washed again in the blood of Jesus. He will
forgive all your mistakes and shortcomings, and look
upon you as though you had never sinned.

The test of true conversion is not your ability to avoid
pitfalls and defeats entirely. It is after you have been

defeated that it becomes apparent whether you have been converted or not. He who honestly goes to God when he has fallen, he is and remains in that holy and child-like fellowship with God into which repentance has brought him.

Nor should you be frightened when your blissful feelings leave you. I know from my own experience how empty and poverty-stricken you feel. But do not think that this has affected your relationship to God. You were received into fellowship with God for *Jesus'* sake; nothing in yourself has made you worthy of such fellowship. And you remain in His fellowship through the merits of Jesus whether you feel happy or sad, as long as you do not by insincerity close your heart to the convicting and admonishing work of the Spirit.

Your life in God does not consist in what you feel. God be praised! Your life in God is deeper than your whole emotional life, and is independent of it. That your life in God affects your emotions is true. Life in God is accompanied by very definite emotions. But not only blissful emotions, as you are so likely to think; but feelings of sorrow, pain, and anxiety as well. All this is an effect of the work of the Spirit of God. Therefore, demand nothing of Him. Permit Him rather to determine from time to time what is best for you, either happy or unhappy feelings, or an utter lack of emotions.

Whatever He works in you He does with the same object in mind: to make you dependent upon the Saviour, clinging to Him and confiding to Him all your experiences.

*

Nor should you give up when you imagine that your life in God is ebbing out, due to the fact that you have no desire for the Word of God or prayer and that

you lust after sin even though you do not dare to prac-
tice it outwardly. You feel like a withered tree, making
a display of dry branches, without the sap and power of
life.

My friend, you are having a hard time of it. This
I know from my own experience. But what you are
now experiencing is not spiritual bankruptcy. The good
work of the Spirit is unquestionably being continued in
your heart. You are in the same situation that Peter was
when Jesus washed his feet: "What I do thou knowest
not now; but thou shalt understand hereafter" (John
13:7).

The Bible says something about God killing and making alive (Deuteronomy 32:39). It also speaks of dying
in order to live with God. In describing his conversion,
Paul says: "I died; and the commandment, which was
unto life, this I found to be unto death" (Romans 7:10).
And Jesus says that as the grain of wheat must fall into
the ground and die before new life can come forth, so
we, too, must lose our life before we can find new life
in God.

You are now experiencing this dying process. And
death is terrible, no matter in what form we meet it. It
is accompanied by both pain and anxiety. Do not permit
yourself to become bewildered on account of this, and
do not permit yourself to be led into believing that you
are not on the right way. It is the Spirit who is doing
His work within you. And He aims at telling you the
truth, the whole, terrible truth about your sinfulness.
And what you have now come to see is the truth: that
you have a heart that does not love God but sin. This
makes you realize how unworthy you are to live in
fellowship with a holy God. This again shows you that

you are a helpless and lost sinner who needs a Saviour. You realize that you are a death-sentenced criminal and you are pleading for mercy.

Has God any way of helping me, you say, with a heart such as I actually have?

Yes. If God could not help you with the heart you have, He would not be able to save sinners at all. No man can change his own worldly, selfish, God-hating heart. God alone can do that. All He wants us to do is to come to Him with our sinful and perverted heart and show it to Him openly and frankly. And the moment we do this, we receive full forgiveness from Him for all our sinfulness, for Jesus' sake.

Very well, you say, but then I should experience some of that change which God has wrought in my heart. But I see nothing of it. It is now a long time since I yielded to God, but my heart is the same: worldly, selfish, with no desire for prayer and the Word of God, but with a terrible lust after sin. Does not that show that God has not changed my heart?

No, by no means! God has, as shown above, already brought about a great change in your attitude (see pages 136 and 137). But it may be that God has not yet finished His work in your heart. And you will have to reconcile yourself to this. He puts to death before He makes alive. He humiliates before He exalts.

Should I not get peace and joy, you ask, if I am truly converted? Many people experience this right after their conversion. Why do not I? Is this not proof that I am not on the right way as far as my conversion is concerned?

In our day it is very natural for this question to become one of the most difficult ones for earnest, seeking souls.

It is in the air, so to speak, and openly stated by many, that if one makes a full surrender to God, one will at once be filled with peace and joy. This view seems to gain verification by the fact that not a few people are given a full measure of blissful emotions immediately after their conversion.

But this is a misunderstanding. Joyous emotions are by no means proof that a person is saved and has been made free in Christ. This is apparent from the fact that these emotions very quickly change into their very opposite, with consequent pain, sorrow, and anxiety. Yet no one on that account would condemn such a person as an apostate.

The emotional aspect must be considered in an entirely different light.

Whether a person after his conversion experiences joyous or distressing feelings, has nothing to do with the genuineness or validity of his conversion. The following apostolic words are applicable here: "The Spirit divides to each one severally even as he will" (I Corinthians 12:11). This is only one stage in the individual's divine up-bringing, and God deals with each one differently, according to his natural proclivities, the particular circumstances surrounding his conversion, and possibly other conditions, which I shall not discuss in detail here.

Surely you must understand that this is something in which you can not meddle. The Lord Himself must decide what is best for you during this early period, whether emotions of joy or of pain.

*

But should not a Christian have assurance, you ask. I have no assurance. I live in a condition of almost ceaseless unrest and uncertainty. Does not that show that there is something wrong with my relationship to God?

Indeed, a Christian should have assurance. But assurance is not a requirement for becoming a Christian. We are saved by faith, not by assurance. Assurance is not a requirement for salvation, but a result of being saved.

To have faith is to come to Christ with your sins and confess them to Him without guile. From that moment a person is saved, no matter whether he feels joy or sorrow. For it is written: "If we confess our sins, he is faithful and righteous to forgive us our sins, and to cleanse us from all unrighteousness" (1 John 1:9). So simple is the way of salvation.

After a person has thus been saved, he receives assurance as an extra gift, in addition to forgiveness. But do not forget that you are to receive it. It is the Holy Spirit who must work assurance in your heart.

What shall I do to receive assurance?

You should first tell God that you have not received assurance as yet and that you are waiting and longing for it. Then you should make use of the means of grace: the Word, prayer, communion, and fellowship (Acts 2:42). Through these means the Spirit will work assurance within you. And, finally, you should leave it to God to decide the time when you are to receive assurance. Do not presume to dictate to God. Furthermore, you need not be afraid to leave that matter with Him. H٠ longs more to give you assurance than you do to receive it.

*

Permit me, in conclusion, to sum up my advice to you who have chosen, but who still find yourself in a great deal of doubt and difficulty: yield yourselves to God. Do not go to God with demands, either for peace, joy, or assurance. Lay everything at the Saviour's feet and say to Him: do with me as Thou deemest best. It is enough for me that Thou wilt save me. Do it in the way that Thou seest best. I have merited nothing, and pray therefore only for grace. And I cling to Thine own words: "He that cometh to me, him will I in no wise cast out."

There is still another little question deep down in your heart which now and then causes you trouble: Why does God proceed in this way? Why does He permit us to grope along in uncertainty instead of giving us what our souls so ardently desire?

Well, God may have various reasons. May I mention only one? That might be reason enough for God to deal with us as He does.

The salvation of a sinner consists in this: God by His Spirit convicts him of sin and leads him to confess his sin humbly and to leave it with God to be wiped out. Now, wilfulness is one of our most deeply rooted and widely prevalent sins. No sin is so hard for us to acknowledge and none harder to give up.

Observe how it follows us into the very presence of God. The sinner has been converted, has yielded to God with his sin and guilt. And this he has done in all earnestness. Notice, however, how wilfulness flourishes in the very presence of God, unacknowledged and unrestrained. Even though the sinner has admitted that he is deserving of death, nevertheless, he presents himself before God with demands. Because he has been so dutiful as to repent, therefore God must give him peace, joy, assurance. And He must do this immediately. And if He does not do so, the sinner feels almost offended!

Is it not true that this is wilfulness of a very unmitigated and unadulterated kind? It appears to me, therefore, that God must convict this sinner also of this great sin. And this He does most easily by delaying the gift which the sinner so impatiently demands. When a sinner gets so far that he sees his wilfulness and surrenders it to God in order to be rid of it, his heart is ready to receive the gifts he is so earnestly striving to get.

My advice is, therefore: acknowledge your impatience and your wilfulness and surrender yourself to God's safe and gracious way of dealing with you. Every time impatience and self-will reasserts itself in your heart, do the same thing again. Then you will experience that God works in you according to His good pleasure. "He who began the good work in you will perfect it until the day of Jesus Christ" (Philippians 1:6).

Do not rest, however, until you receive assurance. Continue in prayer, and wait patiently for Him. "Faithful is he that calleth you, who will also do it" (I Thessalonians 5:24).